caring for... series

Skill-Building Journal

caring for
infants &
toddlers second edition

Derry G. Koralek

with Amy Laura Dombro and Diane Trister Dodge

Teaching Strategies Inc.

Washington, DC

Editors: Laurie Taub, Sherrie Rudick
Cover, book design, and computer illustrations: Carla Uriona
Production: Jennifer Love King

Teaching Strategies, Inc.
P.O. Box 42243
Washington, DC 20015
www.TeachingStrategies.com
ISBN: 978-1-879537-50-7

Teaching Strategies and *The Creative Curriculum* names and logos are
registered trademarks of Teaching Strategies, Inc., Washington, DC.

The publisher and the authors cannot be held responsible for injury,
mishap, or damages incurred during the use of or because of the
information in this book. The authors recommend appropriate and
reasonable supervision at all times based on the age and capability
of each child.

Library of Congress Control Number: 2005924654

Printed and bound in the United States of America
2011   2010   2009
10 9 8 7 6 5 4

Table of Contents

Orientation

Welcome to *Caring for Infants & Toddlers*, a personalized training program designed for teachers who work with infants and toddlers. Whether you are new to the profession or have years of experience, this program offers practical information about topics central to your work. The training program consists of two books: *Caring for Infants & Toddlers* and a *Skill-Building Journal*. This book, *Caring for Infants & Toddlers*, contains all of the readings for the 13 modules in the training program. It also includes a glossary of terms used throughout the training, a list of references, and a bibliography of additional resources. The *Skill-Building Journal* is a personal record of your learning. It includes the instructions and forms for the activities you will do to apply what you have read about each topic and to reflect on your practice.

Early childhood educators who work with infants and toddlers refer to and think of themselves in many ways. They may be called *teacher*, *caregiver*, *care provider*, or even *educarer*. We use the term *teacher* to mean any adult who works with young children in a classroom setting, including mentor teachers, lead teachers, teacher aides, teacher assistants, caregivers, care providers, and volunteers. We use the term *trainer* to refer to the individual who is guiding your participation in this training program.

Several features of *Caring for Infants & Toddlers* make it unique:

- The materials are appropriate for both **new and experienced** teachers.

- You take **responsibility** for your progress through the training program, with **guidance and feedback** provided by a trainer.

- The training program is **individualized**. You work independently, according to your own schedule and at your own pace.

- The information presented in the modules is **practical** and of **immediate use** in your daily work with children.

- Many of the learning activities ask you to **observe** children to learn about their skills and interests. Observation is a key way to get to know children and to plan a program that responds to each child's individual skills, needs, interests, and other characteristics.

- Your completed learning activity forms become a **professional resource** and a record of your growth and competence.

How the Training Program Can Help You

Caring for Infants & Toddlers is designed to help you gain the knowledge and skills to provide a high-quality program for infants and toddlers. The modules describe the typical developmental stages of children from birth to age three and include many examples of how you can apply this knowledge every day in your work. Once you begin this training program, you will discover that you already have many skills and that completing the modules will let you extend your skills and knowledge. The training will help you to meet the profession's standards and to become a more competent teacher.

Completing *Caring for Infants & Toddlers* can help you meet the requirements for achieving a nationally recognized credential that acknowledges your skills as a teacher of infants and toddlers. The training program is based on the Child Development Associate (CDA) Competency Standards defined by The Council for Professional Recognition (the Council) in Washington, DC. The 13 CDA functional areas define the skills and knowledge base of competent teachers.

Functional Areas of the Child Development Associate (CDA) Competency Standards

Safe
Provide a safe environment to prevent and reduce injuries.

Healthy
Promote good health and nutrition and provide an environment that contributes to the prevention of illness.

Learning Environment
Use space, relationships, materials, and routines as resources for constructing an interesting, secure, and enjoyable environment that encourages play, exploration, and learning.

Physical
Provide a variety of equipment, activities, and opportunities to promote the physical development of children.

Cognitive
Provide activities and opportunities that encourage curiosity, exploration, and problem-solving appropriate to the developmental levels and learning styles of children.

Communication
Communicate with children and provide opportunities and support for children to understand, acquire, and use verbal and nonverbal means of communicating thoughts and feelings.

Creative
Provide opportunities that stimulate children to play with sound, rhythm, language, materials, space, and ideas in individual ways to express their creative abilities.

Self
Provide physical and emotional security for each child and help each child to know, accept, and take pride in himself or herself and to develop a sense of independence.

Social
Help each child to feel accepted in the group, help children learn to communicate and get along with others, and encourage feelings of empathy and mutual respect among children and adults.

Guidance
Provide a supportive environment in which children can begin to learn and practice appropriate and acceptable behaviors as individuals and as a group.

Families
Maintain an open, friendly, and cooperative relationship with each child's family, encourage their involvement in the program, and support the child's relationship with his or her family.

Program Management
Use all available resources to ensure an effective operation.

Professionalism
Make decisions based on knowledge of early childhood theories and practices, promote quality in child care services, and take advantage of opportunities to improve competence both for personal and professional growth and for the benefit of children and families.

Each of the modules in *Caring for Infants & Toddlers* addresses one of the CDA functional areas. Teachers may apply for a CDA credential from the Council when they have completed 120 clock hours of training and can demonstrate that they have acquired the skills and knowledge outlined in the CDA Competency Standards. Contact the Council at www.cdacouncil.org or 1-800-424-4310 for more information about the requirements for a CDA credential.

Working With Your Trainer

An important part of the training process is the feedback and support you receive from a trainer. Your trainer might be a colleague, mentor teacher, supervisor, education coordinator, college instructor, or other individual who can observe you working with children and provide meaningful feedback to support your professional development. Although the modules are meant to be self-instructional, you will benefit most if an experienced trainer reviews and discusses your responses to learning activities, answers questions, and comments on your interactions with children and families. Your trainer can provide feedback on-site at the program, during a phone conference, via electronic mail (e-mail), or in a group meeting.

Beginning the Program

After reading this *Orientation*, your next step is to complete the *Self-Assessment* in this *Skill-Building Journal* (section 0-1). The *Self-Assessment* lists the three major areas of competence related to the topic of each module. You read each item and check the box that describes your current level of implementation. You will want to respond as objectively as possible, so you can identify your strengths and interests as well as areas that need strengthening. Afterward, you discuss your responses with your trainer and choose three modules to work on first.

You and your trainer will also develop a tentative schedule for completing the entire training program. You can expect to spend about 4–6 weeks on each module. It generally takes 12–18 months to complete the entire training program.

You might begin with a module of particular interest precisely because you think you have already acquired many of the relevant skills. Alternatively, you might begin with a module that addresses a training need identified through the *Self-Assessment* or your trainer's observations. If this training program is part of a course or seminar, your trainer might ask you to begin with a particular module so you can participate in group meetings with others working on the same module. Your program director might ask you to begin with a module that addresses a program need, such as improving partnerships with families.

Completing Each Module

Each of the 13 modules follows a consistent format using both books. The chart that follows shows how the sections of the books are related.

Section	Caring for Infants & Toddlers	Skill-Building Journal
Overview	An introduction to the topic addressed in the module, identification of three major areas of competence, related strategies, and three brief examples of how teachers apply their knowledge and skills to support children's development and learning.	Questions about each of the examples and sample answers.
Your Own Experiences	A short discussion of how the topic applies to adults.	A series of questions about personal experiences related to the topic.
Pre-Training Assessment (presented only in the *Skill-Building Journal*)		A checklist of how often teachers use key strategies and a question about skills to improve or topics to learn more about.
Learning Activities (4–5 per module)	Objectives for each *Learning Activity* and several pages of information about the topic.	Instructions for applying the reading to classroom practices. This may involve answering questions; observing children and using the information to address individual needs and interests; completing a checklist; trying new teaching strategies; or planning, implementing, and evaluating a new activity. When appropriate, *Answer Sheets* are provided.
Reflecting on Your Learning (presented only in the *Skill-Building Journal*)		An opportunity to consider how the topic relates to curriculum implementation and building partnerships with families. Questions help teachers summarize what they learned.

As you can see from the chart, the two books are coordinated. Each section of a *Caring for Infants & Toddlers* module includes an instruction that directs you to the corresponding section of the *Skill-Building Journal*. Look for the *what's next?* box at the bottom of the page. Similarly, each section of the *Skill-Building Journal* explains whether to continue with the next section of the *Journal* or to return to your reading of *Caring for Infants & Toddlers*.

When you are directed to a section of the *Skill-Building Journal*, you can identify the correct forms by finding the corresponding section numbers in the upper right-hand corner of the pages. The first part of the section number (to the left of the hyphen) indicates the number of the module. The second part of the number (to the right of the hyphen) indicates the step of the module that you are working on. If the step has more than one form, a lowercase letter has been added.

Although the content and activities in the modules vary, you will follow the same process for completing each module. That process is described in the following paragraphs and illustrated in the diagram on page x. As you complete each step, be sure to record your feedback sources in section 1 of each *Skill-Building Journal* module.

Overview

You will read a short introduction to the topic addressed in the module. For each related area of competence, you also review strategies that teachers use and three stories about how they apply their knowledge and skills. Then you answer questions about each story and compare your answers to those on the *Answer Sheet* at the end of the module in the *Skill-Building Journal*.

Your Own Experiences

Next, you will read about how the topic relates to adults and answer questions about how it relates to your own experiences, both on and off the job. You examine how personal experiences affect your approach to your work with children and families and your choice of teaching strategies.

Pre-Training Assessment

The next step is to complete the *Pre-Training Assessment*—a list of the strategies that competent teachers use—by indicating whether you do these things regularly, sometimes, or not enough. Then you will review your responses and identify 3–5 skills you want to improve or topics you want to know learn more about. You may refer to the *Glossary* at the end of *Caring for Infants & Toddlers* for definitions of the terms used.

Next, you will want to schedule a meeting with your trainer to discuss your responses to the *Overview* questions and *Pre-Training Assessment*. After your discussion, you will be ready to begin the learning activities for the module.

Learning Activities

Each module includes four or five learning activities. After reading several pages of information about the topic, you will apply your knowledge while working with children and families. For example, you might answer questions related to the reading and to your own teaching practices; complete a checklist; try out suggestions from the reading and report the results; plan, implement, and evaluate an activity; or observe and record children's behavior and interactions and then use your observation notes to individualize the program. Examples of completed forms, summaries, and charts are provided, when needed, to demonstrate the activity.

Your trainer will be an important source of support as you complete the learning activities. Your trainer might observe the way you implement an activity, conduct a co-observation of a child, review your plans and help you collect materials, or discuss and answer your questions about the content.

After you have completed a learning activity, schedule a time to meet with your trainer, individually or with a group of teachers who completed the same activity. This will be an opportunity to discuss the content of the module, report what you did and learned, and voice your concerns. For some activities, you will also meet with colleagues or a child's family, or review an *Answer Sheet* at the end of the module. It is always best to discuss your work on a learning activity while it is fresh in your mind, so it is important to let your trainer know when you are ready for a feedback conference. A full understanding of each activity is particularly important when an activity builds on the knowledge and skills addressed in the previous one.

Reflecting on Your Learning

After completing all of the learning activities, take time to summarize your progress. Review your responses to the *Pre-Training Assessment* and describe your increased knowledge and skills. For some modules, you will also review and add examples to a chart created in one of the learning activities.

After summarizing your progress, you will meet with your trainer to review your learning and to discuss whether you are ready for the knowledge and competency assessments. When you are ready, schedule a time to complete the *Knowledge Assessment* and set another time for your trainer to conduct the *Competency Assessment* observation. If you need more time to learn about the knowledge and skills addressed in the module, your trainer can suggest supplemental strategies and resources. *Caring for Infants & Toddlers* also includes a bibliography of resources for early childhood professionals.

Assessing Knowledge and Competence

There is a *Knowledge Assessment* for each module and a *Competency Assessment* for modules 1–12. The *Knowledge Assessment* is a short written test about information presented in the modules. For the *Competency Assessment*, your trainer will conduct a focused observation of how you apply your knowledge and use key skills in your work with children. You will need to achieve a score of 80% or higher on each assessment before starting another module. Your trainer will discuss the assessment process in greater detail.

Documenting Progress

As you successfully complete each section and assessment for a module, you can record your progress on the Individual Tracking Form that your trainer will provide and sign.

What's Next
Review *The Training Process* chart that follows, and then complete section 0-1 (*Self Assessment*) in this *Journal*.

The Training Process

Complete the Orientation

Read about the training program
Complete the Self-Assessment
Develop a module-completion plan

Feedback
and
Discussion

Complete a Module

Overview

Read about the topic and three related areas of competence
Review examples of what teachers do
Answer questions

Your Own Experiences

Relate topic to own experiences
Answer questions

Pre-Training Assessment

Assess own use of strategies
List skills to improve or topics to learn about

Learning Activities

Read about topic
Apply knowledge
Answer questions

Reflecting on Your Learning

Review responses to Pre-Training Assessment
Summarize skills and knowledge gained
Discuss readiness for assessments

Feedback
and
Discussion

Not ready for assessment
Review or repeat activities

Ready for assessment
Schedule times

Assessments

Knowledge Assessment
Competency Assessment

Feedback
and
Discussion

Did not demonstrate competence
Review or repeat activities

Demonstrated competence
Document progress
Begin next module

Orientation

Self-Assessment

Competencies

check the appropriate box   *regularly*   *sometimes*   *not enough*

1. Safe

- Maintaining practices and environments that prevent and reduce injuries   ☐ ☐ ☐
- Planning for and responding to emergencies   ☐ ☐ ☐
- Showing children that they are in a safe place   ☐ ☐ ☐

2. Healthy

- Creating and maintaining indoor and outdoor environments that promote wellness   ☐ ☐ ☐
- Using daily routines to introduce good health and nutrition to infants and toddlers   ☐ ☐ ☐
- Recognizing and reporting child abuse and neglect   ☐ ☐ ☐

3. Learning Environment

- Creating indoor and outdoor spaces that support relationships and encourage exploration   ☐ ☐ ☐
- Selecting and arranging equipment and materials that promote development and learning   ☐ ☐ ☐
- Planning daily routines and a flexible schedule that meet each child's needs   ☐ ☐ ☐

4. Physical

- Creating indoor and outdoor environments that invite infants and toddlers to move and explore   ☐ ☐ ☐
- Offering opportunities for infants and toddlers to use their muscles   ☐ ☐ ☐
- Responding as infants and toddlers practice and gain new physical skills   ☐ ☐ ☐

5. Cognitive

- Creating an environment that invites infants and toddlers to learn by using their senses and moving their bodies   ☐ ☐ ☐
- Offering opportunities for infants and toddlers to explore and begin to understand their world   ☐ ☐ ☐
- Interacting with infants and toddlers in ways that encourage them to explore   ☐ ☐ ☐

Competencies, continued

check the appropriate box — regularly / sometimes / not enough

6. Communication

- Creating places where infants and toddlers can enjoy sounds, language, pictures, and print ☐ ☐ ☐
- Offering opportunities for infants and toddlers to explore sounds, language, pictures, and print ☐ ☐ ☐
- Encouraging and responding to infants' and toddlers' efforts to communicate ☐ ☐ ☐

7. Creative

- Creating an environment that encourages exploration and experimentation ☐ ☐ ☐
- Offering opportunities for children to do things in unique ways ☐ ☐ ☐
- Appreciating each child's way of being creative ☐ ☐ ☐

8. Self

- Helping children learn about themselves and others ☐ ☐ ☐
- Providing experiences that allow children to be successful ☐ ☐ ☐
- Building supportive relationships with individual children ☐ ☐ ☐

9. Social

- Creating an environment that helps children develop social skills ☐ ☐ ☐
- Providing opportunities for children to enjoy and appreciate other people ☐ ☐ ☐
- Helping children get along with each other ☐ ☐ ☐

10. Guidance

- Providing an environment that supports the development of self-control ☐ ☐ ☐
- Helping children understand and manage their feelings ☐ ☐ ☐
- Using positive guidance to help children gain self-control ☐ ☐ ☐

Orientation
Self-Assessment, continued

Competencies, continued

check the
appropriate box — regularly / sometimes / not enough

11. Families

- Developing a caregiving partnership with each family   ☐ ☐ ☐
- Offering a variety of ways for families to be involved in the program   ☐ ☐ ☐
- Providing support to families   ☐ ☐ ☐

12. Program Management

- Learning about each child   ☐ ☐ ☐
- Working as a team to offer a program that meets each child's needs   ☐ ☐ ☐
- Evaluating the program   ☐ ☐ ☐

13. Professionalism

- Continually improving your performance   ☐ ☐ ☐
- Continuing to gain new knowledge and skills   ☐ ☐ ☐
- Behaving ethically in your work   ☐ ☐ ☐

Feedback

You will use this *Feedback Summary* many times as you complete the sections of this module. Feedback is an important part of this training program because it helps you check your understanding, apply knowledge, and build skills. You may seek feedback from your colleagues, your trainer, or members of a child's family. When *Answer Sheets* are provided, you may also compare your ideas to example answers. Remember that there can be more than one good answer to a question.

This chart lists some feedback sources and provides space for notes. Each time you get feedback, describe, in the appropriate column, how it was provided (e.g., discussing your responses to learning activities, feedback after your interactions with children have been observed, written comments). This will help you remember to get feedback from a variety of sources and in a number of ways.

Section	Source of Feedback				
	Colleague	**Trainer**	**Child's Family**	**Answer Sheet**	**Other**
Overview					
Your Own Need For Safety					
Pre-Training Assessment					
A. Using Your Knowledge of Infants and Toddlers to Ensure Their Safety					
B. Creating and Maintaining a Safe Environment					
C. Preparing for and Handling Emergencies					
D. Introducing Safety Practices to Children					
Reflecting on Your Learning					

1 Safe

Overview

☐ **Answer** the following questions about the three *Overview* stories in module 1 of *Caring for Infants & Toddlers.*

☐ **Compare** your answers to those on the *Answer Sheet* provided in section 1-10.

☐ **Share and get feedback** on your responses. **Chart** your feedback in section 1-1.

When you are finished, read *Your Own Need for Safety* in module 1 of *Caring for Infants & Toddlers.*

Maintaining Practices and Environments That Prevent and Reduce Injuries

Ms. Gonzalez Acts Quickly

1. What did Ms. Gonzalez do in response to Mr. Lewis's alert and to prevent an injury?

2. What do you think Zora learned from this experience?

Planning for and Responding to Emergencies

Rolling to Safety

1. How did the teachers work together to get the infants out of the building?

2. Why was it necessary for Sammy to wait for his teachers' attention?

Showing Children That They Are in a Safe Place

Ms. Bates Helps Adam Learn About Safety

1. How did Ms. Bates let the children know that they are in a safe place?

2. What did the children learn to do to keep themselves safe?

Your Own Need for Safety

☐ **Think** about a situation in which you were doing something that was potentially dangerous.

☐ **Answer** the following questions about the situation.

☐ **Share and get feedback** on your responses. **Chart** your feedback in section 1-1.

When you are finished, complete section 1-4, *Pre-Training Assessment*.

Describe a situation in which you did not feel safe.

What did you do to prevent or reduce an injury or illness?

What did you learn from this experience that will help you keep children safe?

Pre-Training Assessment

☐ **Read** this list of strategies that teachers use to keep infants and toddlers safe. Refer to the glossary in *Caring for Infants & Toddlers* if you need definitions of the terms that are used.

☐ **Record** whether you do these things *regularly*, *sometimes*, or *not enough*, by checking the appropriate boxes below.

☐ **Review** your answers.

☐ **List** 3–5 skills you would like to improve or topics you would like to learn more about. (When you finish this module, you will list examples of your new or improved understanding and skills.)

☐ **Share and get feedback** on your responses. **Chart** your feedback in section 1-1.

When you are finished, begin *Learning Activity A, Using Your Knowledge of Infants and Toddlers to Ensure Their Safety*, in module 1 of *Caring for Infants & Toddlers*.

Maintaining Practices and Environments That Prevent and Reduce Injuries

check the appropriate box — *regularly* / *sometimes* / *not enough*

1. Check indoor and outdoor areas, toys, materials, and equipment daily and address identified hazards. ☐ ☐ ☐

2. Keep potentially dangerous items and substances out of children's reach at all times. ☐ ☐ ☐

3. Check safety equipment monthly to ensure that it is in good condition and easy for adults to reach. ☐ ☐ ☐

4. Arrange the room with clear exits, pathways, and areas where children can move without bumping into anything. ☐ ☐ ☐

5. Work with colleagues to supervise all children at all times. ☐ ☐ ☐

Pre-Training Assessment, continued

Planning for and Responding to Emergencies

check the appropriate box — regularly / sometimes / not enough

6. Maintain current medical information for all children. ☐ ☐ ☐

7. Respond quickly and calmly to children in distress. ☐ ☐ ☐

8. Develop and post injury and emergency procedures and evacuation routes. ☐ ☐ ☐

9. Make sure a telephone is easy to reach and working properly. ☐ ☐ ☐

10. Check the first-aid kit and safety devices regularly and restock or repair them as needed. ☐ ☐ ☐

11. Know and follow established procedures for taking children to safety during fire and other hazard drills and in real emergencies. ☐ ☐ ☐

Showing Children That They Are in a Safe Place

check the appropriate box — regularly / sometimes / not enough

12. Explain to children what you are doing while taking safety precautions. ☐ ☐ ☐

13. Use positive guidance strategies to redirect children from unsafe to safe activities. ☐ ☐ ☐

14. Model ways to stay safe throughout the day. ☐ ☐ ☐

15. Introduce a few important safety rules to toddlers. ☐ ☐ ☐

16. Share information with families so they can promote their children's safety. ☐ ☐ ☐

Skills to Improve or Topics to Learn More About

Learning Activity A

Using Your Knowledge of Infants and Toddlers to Ensure Their Safety

☐ **Read** the following chart that lists some typical characteristics of young infants, mobile infants, and toddlers that are important to consider when you are ensuring children's safety.

☐ **Write** examples of things you do to ensure children's safety that correspond with these characteristics. You might describe how you arrange furniture, provide toys and materials, handle routines, interact with infants and toddlers, and partner with families. If you need help getting started, turn to the completed chart in section 1-10.

☐ **Share and get feedback** on your responses. **Chart** your feedback in section 1-1.

☐ **Add** more examples to the chart as you complete the rest of the learning activities in this module and learn more about keeping children safe.

When you are finished, begin *Learning Activity B, Creating and Maintaining a Safe Environment*, in module 1 of *Caring for Infants & Toddlers*.

Using Your Knowledge of Young Infants (Birth–8 Months)

Young Infants ...	What I Do to Ensure Young Infants' Safety
put almost everything they hold into their mouths	*Keep small, easily swallowed objects out of infants' reach. Make sure toys do not have pieces that might break off and cause infants to choke. Remove toys with toxic paint.*
wiggle and squirm, sometimes unexpectedly	
roll over, from back to stomach and stomach to back	
sit on a blanket or rug, propped at first and then without external support	
touch, pat, and then hold their bottles	
reach for things they see	

Using Your Knowledge of Mobile Infants (8–18 Months)

Mobile Infants . . .	What I Do to Ensure Mobile Infants' Safety
move by creeping and crawling	*Provide protected areas for children who creep and crawl so they won't be trampled by children who are starting to walk. Keep potentially dangerous objects (such as plastic bags and scissors) out of reach.*
explore objects by grabbing, throwing, shaking, dumping, and dropping	
understand many words and follow simple directions	
pull themselves up to a standing position	
enjoy taking part in daily routines and activities	
begin to walk on their own	

Using Your Knowledge of Toddlers (18–36 Months)

Toddlers ...	What I Do to Ensure Toddlers' Safety
love to run but cannot always stop or turn	*Provide open spaces that are carpeted or grassy enough to cushion falls. Make sure floor coverings are secured. Pick up toys toddlers may trip on. Remind toddlers to slow down and watch where they are going.*
understand rules but need to be reminded to follow them	
enjoy climbing—on anything and everything	
act on their curiosity by manipulating, poking, handling, twisting, and squeezing objects	
push, pull, and ride wheeled toys	
like to imitate their favorite grown-ups	

From *Skill-Building Journal for Caring for Infants & Toddlers, Module 1, Safe.*
©2005 Teaching Strategies, Inc., Washington, DC 20015, www.TeachingStrategies.com

☐ **Read** the safety practices and precautions on the daily and monthly safety checklists that follow.

☐ **Review** the safety charts in *Learning Activity B* of *Caring for Infants & Toddlers*. From the charts, **select** additional safety practices and precautions that are relevant to the indoor and outdoor spaces in which you care for infants and toddlers. **Discuss** your selections with a colleague and **decide** whether to check these items daily or monthly.

☐ **Add** the practices and precautions you selected to the daily and weekly safety checklists. This will allow you to create safety checklists that meet your program's needs. **Print** the form and use more paper if needed.

☐ **Assess** the safety of your indoor and outdoor spaces by using the daily and monthly checklists you created.

☐ **Review** your findings and address any potential hazards. **Record** your plans on the "Summary of Checklist Findings" that follows the checklists.

☐ **Discuss** your creation and use of these safety checklists with your colleagues. **Work** as a team to finalize the checklists and to establish a system and schedule for using them. **Chart** your feedback in section 1-1.

When you are finished, begin *Learning Activity C, Preparing for and Handling Emergencies*, in module 1 of *Caring for Infants & Toddlers*.

Daily Safety Checklist

Center-Wide

check the appropriate box — satisfactory/ not applicable — needs attention

1. Supervise all children, at all times and in all areas. ☐ ☐
2. Make sure the sign-in/sign-out log is in a designated place with a supply of pens. ☐ ☐
3. Cover unused electrical outlets. ☐ ☐
4. ☐ ☐
5. ☐ ☐
6. ☐ ☐
7. ☐ ☐
8. ☐ ☐

Toys, Furniture, and Equipment

check the appropriate box — satisfactory/ not applicable — needs attention

9. Display heavy toys on bottom shelves. ☐ ☐
10. Use protective corners or edge bumpers on furniture with sharp edges at children's eye level. ☐ ☐
11. Place cushioning under indoor climbers. ☐ ☐
12. ☐ ☐
13. ☐ ☐
14. ☐ ☐
15. ☐ ☐
16. ☐ ☐

Daily Safety Checklist, continued

Emergency Preparedness

check the appropriate box

	satisfactory/ not applicable	needs attention
17. Make sure emergency exits are clear and unlocked from inside.	☐	☐
18.	☐	☐
19.	☐	☐
20.	☐	☐
21.	☐	☐
22.	☐	☐

Storage

check the appropriate box

	satisfactory/ not applicable	needs attention
23. Store adult purses, tote bags, and plastic bags out of children's reach.	☐	☐
24. Keep cleaning supplies in locked cabinets.	☐	☐
25.	☐	☐
26.	☐	☐
27.	☐	☐
28.	☐	☐
29.	☐	☐

Daily Safety Checklist, continued

Outdoors

check the appropriate box

	satisfactory/ not applicable	needs attention
30. Check the area for glass, nails, and other debris.	☐	☐
31. Check for standing water.	☐	☐
32.	☐	☐
33.	☐	☐
34.	☐	☐
35.	☐	☐
36.	☐	☐

Transportation

check the appropriate box

	satisfactory/ not applicable	needs attention
37. Install safety seats properly.	☐	☐
38.	☐	☐
39.	☐	☐
40.	☐	☐
41.	☐	☐
42.	☐	☐

Monthly Safety Checklist

Center-Wide

check the appropriate box — satisfactory/ not applicable — needs attention

	satisfactory/ not applicable	needs attention
1. Electrical cords are not frayed or damaged.	☐	☐
2. Covers and insulation on radiators and pipes are in good repair.	☐	☐
3. All items are free from protruding nails, splinters, cracks, chipped paint, and lead paint. Nuts, bolts, and screws are secure.	☐	☐
4.	☐	☐
5.	☐	☐
6.	☐	☐
7.	☐	☐
8.	☐	☐

Toys, Furniture, and Equipment

check the appropriate box — satisfactory/ not applicable — needs attention

	satisfactory/ not applicable	needs attention
9. Safety straps on equipment are in good repair.	☐	☐
10. Cribs are in good repair.	☐	☐
11. Toys are in good repair.	☐	☐
12.	☐	☐
13.	☐	☐
14.	☐	☐
15.	☐	☐
16.	☐	☐

SECTION **1-6f**

Learning Activity B, continued
Creating and Maintaining a Safe Environment

Monthly Safety Checklist, continued

Emergency Preparedness

check the appropriate box — satisfactory/not applicable — needs attention

17. An emergency evacuation drill is conducted monthly. ☐ ☐

18. Smoke detectors are functioning. ☐ ☐

19. ☐ ☐

20. ☐ ☐

21. ☐ ☐

22. ☐ ☐

23. ☐ ☐

Storage

check the appropriate box — satisfactory/not applicable — needs attention

24. Locks on cabinets are working. ☐ ☐

25. ☐ ☐

26. ☐ ☐

27. ☐ ☐

28. ☐ ☐

29. ☐ ☐

From *Skill-Building Journal for Caring for Infants & Toddlers, Module 1, Safe.*
©2005 Teaching Strategies, Inc., Washington, DC 20015, www.TeachingStrategies.com

Monthly Safety Checklist, continued

Outdoors

check the appropriate box — *satisfactory/ not applicable* — *needs attention*

30. Play equipment is in good repair. ☐ ☐

31. Cushioning under and around equipment meets safety standards. ☐ ☐

32. ☐ ☐

33. ☐ ☐

34. ☐ ☐

35. ☐ ☐

36. ☐ ☐

Transportation

check the appropriate box — *satisfactory/ not applicable* — *needs attention*

37. Children's emergency information is current. ☐ ☐

38. ☐ ☐

39. ☐ ☐

40. ☐ ☐

41. ☐ ☐

42. ☐ ☐

Learning Activity B, continued
Creating and Maintaining a Safe Environment

Summary of Checklist Findings

Practice/Precaution	Response	Who	When

Date to use the Monthly Safety Checklist again: _____

Learning Activity C
Preparing for and Handling Emergencies

☐ **Read** your program's emergency plan (the written document that describes how to respond when children are injured or ill and when it is necessary to evacuate the center because of a fire or other crisis).

☐ **Answer** the questions that follow. **Refer** to your program's emergency plan if necessary.

☐ **Share and get feedback** on your responses. **Chart** your feedback in section 1-1.

When you are finished, begin *Learning Activity D, Introducing Safety Practices to Children*, in module 1 of *Caring for Infants & Toddlers*.

Emergency Plans

Injuries

1. A mobile infant accidentally steps on the hand of a crawling infant, leaving a bruise. What would you do?

   How and when would the child's family be notified about this minor injury?

2. While you are with a small group at a nearby park, a toddler has a severe reaction to a bee sting. What would you do?

   How and when would you notify your supervisor and the child's family?

3. What medical facility does your program use? How would a seriously injured or ill child get there? Who would go with the child?

Evacuating the Center

1. How do you lead your group of infants and toddlers to safety during an emergency evacuation?

   What would you do if the planned route were blocked?

   What phone number would you use to call for assistance?

2. What would you do if you smelled smoke?

Natural Disasters and Weather-Related Emergencies

1. What potentially dangerous weather conditions and other natural disasters occur in your area?

2. Describe your program's plans for responding during one of these emergencies.

☐ **Read** the example that follows.

☐ **Observe** children during a routine or activity (e.g., outdoor play or eating) during which older infants and toddlers can begin to learn about safety. **Tell** your colleagues that you will be observing one of them with a child.

☐ **Take notes** about what you observe, during or right after your observation.

☐ **Review** your notes and think about what the child might have been experiencing and learning. Use your notes to **answer** the questions that follow.

☐ **Share and get feedback** on your responses. **Chart** your feedback in section 1-1.

When you are finished, complete section 1-9, *Reflecting on Your Learning*.

Observing Children as They Learn About Safety—Example

Routine or Activity: _Diapering_   **Date:** _November 11_

Child(ren)/Age(s): _Andrew (28 months)_

Colleague: _Mr. Lewis_

Observation Notes:

Andrew tugs on diaper and says, "Wet!" Mr. Lewis lifts Andrew onto diapering table and has him lie down. Andrew wiggles and squirms. Mr. L. says, "Remember, Andrew, you have to stay still so you won't fall and get hurt." Andrew stops kicking. Mr. L. smiles and says, "Thanks for helping, Andrew. Staying still helps keep you safe." Mr. L. and Andrew talk and laugh.

Consider the experience through the eyes of the child(ren). Use your imagination to describe what the child(ren) might be feeling, thinking, and learning.

I don't like having a wet diaper, so I am moving around. I forgot to stay still. Mr. Lewis smiled when I stopped kicking. It must be a good thing to do.

What potential hazards did you identify?

A child could fall from the changing table if an adult were not present to keep him from rolling off. A teacher could pull a muscle while lifting a toddler onto and off of the changing table.

How else could you and your colleagues introduce safety during this routine or activity?

We could build sturdy steps at the foot of the diapering table so toddlers like Andrew can climb up without being lifted.

Observing Children as They Learn About Safety

Routine or Activity: _____   **Date:** _____

Child(ren)/Age(s): _____

Colleague: _____

Observation Notes:

Consider the experience through the eyes of the child(ren). Use your imagination to describe what the child(ren) might be feeling, thinking, and learning.

What potential hazards did you identify?

How else could you and your colleagues introduce safety during this routine or activity?

Reflecting on Your Learning

You have now completed all of the learning activities for this module. Whether you are a new or experienced teacher, you have gained new understandings and developed new skills for ensuring the safety of infants and toddlers. Before going on to the next module, take a few minutes to think about what you have learned. As you complete the steps below, chart your feedback in section 1-1.

☐ **Review the chart** you completed in *Learning Activity A, Using Your Knowledge of Infants and Toddlers to Ensure Their Safety.* Think about the new ideas you learned as you completed the learning activities in this module. **Add to the chart** examples of things you did while working on this module to maintain a safe environment for infants and toddlers.

☐ **Review your responses** to the *Pre-Training Assessment* for this module and **complete** section 1-9b, "Summarizing Progress."

☐ **Explore some curriculum connections.** You will use what you learned in module 1, *Safe*, when implementing a curriculum. Look through your program's curriculum to see how it addresses this topic. For example, *The Creative Curriculum® for Infants & Toddlers* has some sections you might want to review:

• Chapter 8, *Ensuring Children's Safety*, and Appendix C, *Safety and Health Checklists*, cover safety topics in depth.

• Chapter 23, *Going Outdoors*, addresses safety problems and solutions in the section "Setting the Stage for Outdoor Play."

☐ **Build partnerships with families.** Share what you learned in this module with the families of children in your care. Here are some suggestions:

• Use the development charts in *Learning Activity A* to discuss ways to promote safety at home.

• Make a handout using the list of prohibited practices ("Nevers") from *Learning Activity B*.

• Regularly share information about product recalls and other safety-related issues that affect infants and toddlers.

• Share other information to help families keep their children safe at home, in vehicles, on the playground, and when walking near busy streets. For example, you can refer them to Web sites such as the National SAFE KIDS Campaign (www.safekids.org) and the American Academy of Pediatrics (www.aap.org).

☐ **Complete the assessments.** Tell the trainer who is guiding you through the modules that you are ready for the knowledge and competency assessments.

☐ **Start a new module.** After completing the assessments successfully, it is time to move on. Congratulations on your progress so far, and good luck with the next module.

Reflecting on Your Learning

Summarizing Progress

Name: _____ **Date:** _____

Did completing this module help you ensure the safety of infants and toddlers? List the strategies you use.

How did you share something you learned with families?

What did you learn about an individual child, and how do you plan to use this information?

What curriculum connections did you explore?

What do you want to learn more about, and how will you do it?

Maintaining Practices and Environments That Prevent and Reduce Injuries

Ms. Gonzalez Acts Quickly

1. What did Ms. Gonzalez do in response to Mr. Lewis's alert and to prevent an injury?
   - *Ms. Gonzalez responded quickly to Mr. Lewis's warning and calmly moved Zora to keep her safe.*
   - *She put the box of balls in the closet so other children wouldn't climb on it.*

2. What do you think Zora learned from this experience?
   - *She can trust Ms. Gonzalez to keep her safe.*
   - *The climber is a safe place for climbing.*
   - *She can help Ms. Gonzalez in a meaningful way to make the room safer.*

Planning for and Responding to Emergencies

Rolling to Safety

1. How did the teachers work together to get the infants out of the building?
   - *They followed the center's established procedures for drills and emergencies.*
   - *They moved quickly and shared responsibility.*
   - *Before going outside, they checked with each other to confirm that they had all of the children.*

2. Why was it necessary for Sammy to wait for his teachers' attention?
   - *The first priority was to get all the infants outside as quickly as possible. Once everyone was safe, the teachers could respond to Sammy.*

Showing Children That They Are In a Safe Place

Ms. Bates Helps Adam Learn About Safety

1. How did Ms. Bates let the children know that they are in a safe place?
   - *She helped Adam learn a safe way to knock down the block tower.*
   - *She modeled asking the other children to move away from the tower before it was knocked down.*

2. What did the children learn to do to keep themselves safe?
   - *They learned how to knock down blocks in a safe way.*
   - *They learned to give a warning to other people and time to move away before they knock down the blocks.*
   - *They learned that there are things they can do to be safe.*

Using Your Knowledge of Young Infants (Birth–8 Months)

Young Infants . . .	What I Do to Ensure Young Infants' Safety
put almost everything they hold into their mouths	*Keep small, easily swallowed objects out of infants' reach. Make sure toys do not have pieces that could break off. Remove toys with toxic paint.*
wiggle and squirm, sometimes unexpectedly	*Dry my hands before picking infants up. Establish emergency evacuation procedures, including the use of rolling cribs, so that I do not need to carry several children at the same time.*
roll over, from back to stomach and stomach to back	*Always stay with infants who are on changing tables. Create a protected area on the floor where infants can play or watch others.*
sit on a blanket or rug, propped at first and then without external support	*Prop up an infant who is just learning to sit. Stay near an unsteady baby who is just learning to sit.*
touch, pat, and then hold their bottles	*Hold infants when feeding them. Never prop bottles for infants because they might choke.*
reach for things they see	*Put safe, interesting objects within infants' reach, but do not hang toys across the cribs of infants who can sit up or push up on their hands and knees. Hang mobiles out of children's reach, and make sure the attached pieces are secure. Carefully examine the rug for fibers and other debris that infants might put in their mouths.*

Using Your Knowledge of Mobile Infants (8–18 Months)

Mobile Infants ...	What I Do to Ensure Mobile Infants' Safety
move by creeping and crawling	*Provide protected areas for children who creep and crawl so they won't be trampled by children who are starting to walk. Keep potentially dangerous objects (such as plastic bags and scissors) out of reach.*
explore objects by grabbing, throwing, shaking, dumping, and dropping	*Keep breakable toys and equipment out of reach. Provide soft objects for throwing games, such as beach balls and small pillows.*
understand many words and follow simple directions	*Introduce a few rules and give frequent reminders because children can't remember and follow them on their own. Use the environment to help set limits. Observe so I know what children are doing and to give them safety reminders as necessary.*
pull themselves up to a standing position	*Cover sharp corners of tables or shelves that infants might bump. Check to be sure shelves and other furniture are stable and will support children's weight. Lower crib mattresses so infants will not fall over the rail. Keep crib sides up.*
enjoy taking part in daily routines and activities	*Offer children opportunities to participate throughout the day. Check equipment regularly so I can replace anything that is not in good condition. Stay alert and ready to guide children's behavior.*
begin to walk on their own	*Provide carpeted and grassy surfaces that cushion falls. Pick up items infants might trip over. Get the attention of a child who is beginning to walk by facing the child when I speak.*

From *Skill-Building Journal for Caring for Infants & Toddlers, Module 1, Safe.*
©2005 Teaching Strategies, Inc., Washington, DC 20015, www.TeachingStrategies.com

Using Your Knowledge of Toddlers (18–36 Months)

Toddlers ...	What I Do to Ensure Toddlers' Safety
love to run but cannot always stop or turn	*Provide open spaces that are carpeted or grassy enough to cushion falls. Make sure floor coverings are secure. Pick up toys toddlers might trip on. Remind toddlers to slow down and watch where they are going.*
understand rules but need to be reminded to follow them	*Discuss rules with toddlers, but be aware that they cannot always remember or follow them. Observe and remind toddlers of ways to stay safe.*
enjoy climbing—on anything and everything	*Be sure that climbing toys are on cushioned surfaces. Provide lots of safe, sturdy climbing equipment and many opportunities for climbing. Remove potentially dangerous climbing structures, such as boxes that will collapse under children's weight.*
act on their curiosity by manipulating, poking, handling, twisting, and squeezing objects	*Cover electrical outlets and exposed radiators. Remove toys and other items with jagged edges or splinters. Keep sharp objects (knives, scissors) out of toddlers' reach. Lock cleaning solutions and medicines in high cabinets. Remove small objects that toddlers could put in mouths, ears, or noses.*
push, pull, and ride wheeled toys	*Let toddlers ride on hard, obstacle-free surfaces. Help children take turns. Talk together about safe riding and enforce the use of helmets. Organize a riding area so riders will not crash into other toddlers.*
like to imitate their favorite grown-ups	*Model safe practices throughout the day. Talk with children about safety practices and why they prevent accidents and injuries. Talk with family members about how they are important safety models at home.*

Feedback

You will use this *Feedback Summary* many times as you complete the sections of this module. Feedback is an important part of this training program because it helps you check your understanding, apply knowledge, and build skills. You may seek feedback from your colleagues, your trainer, or members of a child's family. When an *Answer Sheet* is provided, you may also compare your ideas to example answers. Remember that there can be more than one good answer to a question.

This chart lists some feedback sources and provides space for notes. Each time you get feedback, describe, in the appropriate column, how it was provided (e.g., discussing your responses to learning activities, feedback after your interactions with children have been observed, written comments). This will help you remember to get feedback from a variety of sources and in a number of ways.

Section	Source of Feedback				
	Colleague	**Trainer**	**Child's Family**	**Answer Sheet**	**Other**
Overview					
Your Own Health and Nutrition					
Pre-Training Assessment					
A. Using Your Knowledge of Infants and Toddlers to Promote Good Health and Nutrition					
B. Creating and Maintaining a Hygienic Environment					
C. Introducing Health and Nutrition to Infants and Toddlers					
D. Recognizing and Reporting the Signs of Child Abuse and Neglect					
Reflecting on Your Learning					

Overview

☐ **Answer** the following questions about the three *Overview* stories in module 2 of **Caring for Infants & Toddlers**.

☐ **Compare** your answers to those on the *Answer Sheet* provided in section 2-10.

☐ **Share and get feedback** on your responses. **Chart** your feedback in section 2-1.

When you are finished, read *Your Own Health and Nutrition* in module 2 of **Caring for Infants & Toddlers**.

Creating and Maintaining Indoor and Outdoor Environments That Promote Wellness

Lovette Wipes Her Own Nose

1. What are three things that Ms. Gonzalez did to maintain an environment that promotes wellness?

2. What did Ms. Gonzalez do to prevent germs from spreading?

Using Daily Routines to Introduce Good Health and Nutrition to Infants and Toddlers

Crunchy Apples and Shiny Teeth

1. What did Mr. Lewis do to help the children develop healthy habits?

2. How did the children use self-help skills during daily routines?

Recognizing and Reporting Child Abuse and Neglect

Noticing Some Unexplained Bruises

1. What signs of possible child abuse and neglect did Ms. Bates observe?

2. How did the center director support Ms. Bates?

Your Own Health and Nutrition

☐ **Think** about your whole state of well-being: physical, mental, social, and emotional.

☐ **Answer** the following questions. Your answers are personal and do not have to be shared with anyone.

When you are finished, complete section 2-4, *Pre-Training Assessment*.

What healthy habits do you want to maintain or improve?

What unhealthy habits do you want to minimize or stop?

How does your overall health affect your work?

What three things will you do to stay healthy or improve your health?

Pre-Training Assessment

☐ **Read** this list of strategies that teachers use to promote infants' and toddlers' health. Refer to the glossary in *Caring for Infants & Toddlers* if you need definitions of the terms that are used.

☐ **Record** whether you do these things *regularly*, *sometimes*, or *not enough*, by checking the appropriate boxes below.

☐ **Review** your answers.

☐ **List** 3–5 skills you would like to improve or topics you would like to learn more about. (When you finish this module, you will list examples of your new or improved knowledge and skills.)

☐ **Share and get feedback** on your responses. **Chart** your feedback in section 2-1.

When you are finished, begin *Learning Activity A, Using Your Knowledge of Infants and Toddlers to Promote Good Health and Nutrition*, in module 2 of *Caring for Infants & Toddlers*.

Creating and Maintaining Indoor and Outdoor Environments That Promote Wellness

check the appropriate box — regularly / sometimes / not enough

	regularly	sometimes	not enough
1. Check the room daily for adequate ventilation and lighting, comfortable temperatures, and sanitary conditions.	☐	☐	☐
2. Arrange the diapering area so it is easy to sanitize.	☐	☐	☐
3. Provide tissues and paper towels where mobile infants and toddlers can reach them.	☐	☐	☐
4. Complete daily health checks and stay alert to symptoms of illness throughout the day.	☐	☐	☐
5. Wash and disinfect toys and surfaces daily.	☐	☐	☐
6. Use the handwashing methods recommended by the American Academy of Pediatrics (AAP) and the American Public Health Association (APHA) to help prevent the spread of germs.	☐	☐	☐

Using Daily Routines to Introduce Good Health and Nutrition to Infants and Toddlers

check the appropriate box — regularly / sometimes / not enough

7. Help children gradually gain self-help skills for toileting, handwashing, toothbrushing, and eating. ☐ ☐ ☐

8. Model and talk about healthy habits such as handwashing, using tissues, eating nutritious foods, and washing and disinfecting materials and surfaces. ☐ ☐ ☐

9. Tell families about how you and your colleagues promote wellness. ☐ ☐ ☐

10. Exchange information with families about their child's health and nutrition. ☐ ☐ ☐

Recognizing and Reporting Child Abuse and Neglect

check the appropriate box — regularly / sometimes / not enough

11. Respond to children in caring ways while avoiding situations that might be questioned by others. ☐ ☐ ☐

12. Know the definitions of physical abuse, physical neglect, sexual abuse, and emotional abuse and neglect. ☐ ☐ ☐

13. Recognize and be alert to the physical and behavioral signs that a child might be a victim of abuse or neglect. ☐ ☐ ☐

14. Report suspected child abuse and neglect to authorities according to applicable laws and program policies. ☐ ☐ ☐

15. Support families by helping them get the services they need. ☐ ☐ ☐

Skills to Improve or Topics to Learn More About

Learning Activity A

Using Your Knowledge of Infants and Toddlers to Promote Good Health and Nutrition

☐ **Read** the following chart that lists some typical characteristics of young infants, mobile infants, and toddlers that are related to health and nutrition.

☐ **Write** examples of things you do to promote health and nutrition that correspond to these characteristics. You might describe how you arrange the environment, provide toys and materials, handle routines, interact with infants and toddlers, and partner with families. If you need help getting started, turn to the completed chart in section 2-10.

☐ **Share and get feedback** on your responses. **Chart** your feedback in section 2-1.

☐ **Add** more examples to the chart as you complete the rest of the learning activities in this module and learn more about keeping infants and toddlers healthy.

When you are finished, begin *Learning Activity B, Creating and Maintaining a Hygienic Environment*, in module 2 of **Caring for Infants & Toddlers**.

Learning Activity A, continued
Using Your Knowledge of Infants and
Toddlers to Promote Good Health and Nutrition

SECTION **2-5b**

Using Your Knowledge of Young Infants (Birth–8 Months)

Young Infants ...	What I Do to Promote Young Infants' Health and Nutrition
have individual schedules for eating, sleeping, and eliminating	*Individualize daily schedules to meet each infant's need for play, rest, eating, and diapering.*
soil and wet their diapers and clothes	
get much of their nutrition by breastfeeding or drinking from bottles	
are developing secure attachments with families and teachers	
use their senses (touch, hearing, sight, taste, and smell) to learn about the world	
have weak neck muscles that cannot immediately support their large, heavy heads	

Using Your Knowledge of Mobile Infants (8–18 Months)

Mobile Infants ...	What I Do to Promote Mobile Infants' Health and Nutrition
pick up small objects by using thumb and forefinger (pincer grasp)	*Offer infants nutritious foods that they can practice picking up and eating by themselves, such as pieces of banana and breadsticks.*
begin to take off hats, shoes, and socks and cooperate when being dressed	
hold toys, cups, and other objects with two hands	
crawl and pull themselves up by holding onto furniture and railings	
understand a few words and simple phrases and sometimes follow simple instructions	
enjoy water play	

Using Your Knowledge of Toddlers (18–36 Months)

Toddlers ...	What I Do to Promote Toddlers' Health and Nutrition
learn self-help skills and use them during routines	*Invite children to participate in daily routines that promote good health, such as dressing to go outdoors and preparing nutritious snacks and meals. Talk about how these activities help people stay healthy.*
gain large motor skills, e.g., running, jumping, kicking, climbing, and throwing	
begin to learn about health and nutrition	
may have strong opinions about foods they like and dislike	
begin to gain some bowel and bladder control	
like to do things for themselves, most of the time	

☐ Use the "Hygienic Environment Checklist" that follows to assess your use of practices that promote wellness and reduce disease.

☐ **Review** the assessment results with your colleagues. Discuss items in need of improvement.

☐ **Develop** a plan for addressing any health practices that need to be improved. Describe the planned response, who is responsible, and when the change will be completed.

☐ **Agree** on a date to use the checklist again and record it on your calendar.

☐ **Share and get feedback** on your response. **Chart** your feedback in section 2-1.

When you are finished, begin *Learning Activity C, Introducing Health and Nutrition to Infants and Toddlers,* in module 2 of **Caring for Infants & Toddlers**.

Hygienic Environment Checklist

Date:_____

Healthy Practices

Center-wide

check the appropriate box — satisfactory — needs attention

		satisfactory	needs attention
1.	Keep the inside air temperature between 65° and 72° F.	☐	☐
2.	Open windows to let in fresh air, unless the air conditioning is on.	☐	☐
3.	Line metal or plastic trash containers in the food preparation, diapering, and toileting areas with large, sturdy plastic bags.	☐	☐
4.	Remove and replace trash bags, daily and more often if needed.	☐	☐
5.	Wear washable smocks and clothing; change clothing if soiled.	☐	☐
6.	Store toothbrushes so they can air dry without touching each other.	☐	☐
7.	Have each child use the toothbrush labeled with his name.	☐	☐
8.	Cover the outdoor sand play area when it is not in use.	☐	☐
9.	Check each child daily for signs of illness.	☐	☐
10.	Take universal blood precautions at all times.	☐	☐

Learning Activity B, continued
Creating and Maintaining a Hygienic Environment

Handwashing

check the appropriate box — satisfactory — needs attention

11. Follow AAP and APHA recommendations for when to wash your hands and children's hands. ☐ ☐

12. Follow AAP and APHA recommendations for how to wash your hands and children's hands. ☐ ☐

Disinfecting

check the appropriate box — satisfactory — needs attention

13. Make fresh bleach solutions daily; store out of direct sunlight and children's reach; discard unused portions. ☐ ☐

14. Keep **surface** bleach solution in labeled spray bottles in kitchen, bathroom, and diapering areas; use to disinfect all surfaces except play materials. ☐ ☐

15. Keep **mild** and **dishwashing** bleach solution in labeled containers; use to disinfect items mouthed by children. ☐ ☐

16. Place toys and other items mouthed by children in a container during the day; clean and disinfect at the end of the day. ☐ ☐

17. Wash cloth toys and books at least weekly. ☐ ☐

Feeding and Eating

check the appropriate box — satisfactory — needs attention

18. Prepare food near a sink in an area used only for bottles and food. ☐ ☐

19. Put baby food in a clean bowl before feeding; discard leftovers. ☐ ☐

20. Disinfect tables, counters, and high chair trays with surface bleach solution before and after snacks, meals, and activities. ☐ ☐

21. Check refrigerator daily to make sure temperature is below 40° F. ☐ ☐

22. Label breast milk, formula bottles, and perishable foods with child's name and date. Refrigerate at 40° F or cooler. ☐ ☐

23. Discard formula left in a bottle after a feeding (do not save for later if the feeding lasted more than one hour) and unused mixed formula after 48 hours. ☐ ☐

24. Have children use their own bottles, bowls, and utensils; return items to kitchen for washing, drying, and disinfection. ☐ ☐

Diapering and Toileting

check the appropriate box | satisfactory | needs attention

25. Change diapers only in the diapering area; follow AAP and APHA procedures. ☐ ☐

26. Use the diapering area for changing diapers and nothing else. ☐ ☐

27. Check diapers at least hourly and change as needed. ☐ ☐

28. Keep the diapering area stocked with supplies. ☐ ☐

29. Store individual supplies in containers labeled with names. ☐ ☐

30. Wash and disinfect bathroom faucet handles, sinks, the floor, and toilet seats at least once a day and when soiled. ☐ ☐

31. Flush potty chair contents in toilet if potty chairs are used; rinse in utility sink; wash and dry with paper towels twice; disinfect; air dry; disinfect sink; wash hands. ☐ ☐

32. Stock the bathroom with disposable wipes, toilet paper, paper towels, and soap. Place these supplies within toddlers' reach. ☐ ☐

Sleeping

check the appropriate box | satisfactory | needs attention

33. Place cribs (unless they have Plexiglas® partitions), mats, cots at least 3' apart and/or lay children head to toe. ☐ ☐

34. Have children sleep in assigned beds with linens from home. ☐ ☐

35. Change blankets at least monthly and sheets at least weekly; also change linens whenever soiled, used by a sick child, or used by another child. Put soiled linens in plastic bags until laundered or sent home. ☐ ☐

Hygienic Environment Checklist

Summary of Findings

On the chart below, list the practices you found to be in need of improvement. Then describe the improvement strategies you plan to use. Note who is responsible and when the strategies will be implemented.

Practices Needing Improvement	Improvement Strategies	Who	When

Date to use Hygienic Environment Checklist again: _____

Learning Activity C
Introducing Health and Nutrition to Infants and Toddlers

☐ **Read** the example that follows, to assist your thinking about routines.

☐ **Observe** a colleague and one or two older infants or toddlers during a daily routine or activity. Let your colleagues **know** you will be conducting this observation.

☐ **Take notes** about your observations, during or right after the observation period.

☐ **Review** your notes and think about what the child(ren) might have been experiencing and learning. **Use** your notes to answer the questions that follow.

☐ **Share and get feedback** on your responses. **Chart** your feedback in section 2-1.

When you are finished, complete *Learning Activity D, Recognizing and Reporting the Signs of Child Abuse and Neglect*, in module 2 of *Caring for Infants & Toddlers*.

Helping Children Learn About Health and Nutrition During Routines—Example

Routine or Activity: _Water play_   **Date:** _April 2_

Colleague: _Ms. Bates_

Child(ren)/Age(s): _Andrea (19 months), Tim (25 months)_

Observation Notes:

Ms. Bates, Andrea, and Tim wash hands. Ms. Bates says, "Now we won't pass our germs to each other when we play in the water." All walk to table, which has two basins of water on top. Children put dolls in water and wash them with soap. Water gets soapy. Tim says, "Bubbles!" Ms. Bates smiles at him and says, "Yes, lots of bubbles." She asks, "Have you cleaned their elbows?" Tim says, "What's that?" Ms. Bates points to her elbow and to the doll's. Tim asks, "These?" Ms. Bates nods. All talk about the body parts of dolls and people. Ms. Bates hands out towels. She says, "Use these to dry your dolls. When we are dry, we don't feel as cold as when we are wet."

Consider the experience from the child(ren)'s point of view. Describe what the child(ren) might have been feeling, thinking, and learning.

Tim: Elbow, elbow, elbow. That's fun to say. I wonder what it is. Oh, here's my elbow.
Andrea: I dry the baby to take care of her, like my daddy takes care of me.

How did your colleague help the child(ren) develop good health habits?

She washed hands with the children before water play.
She introduced Tim to the name for a part of the body: elbow.
She talked with them about the names of other body parts.
She offered towels so they could dry the dolls and explained that people feel warmer when they are dry.
She provided a way for them to pretend to care for babies in a way that grown-ups care for them.

Helping Children Learn About Health and Nutrition During Routines

Routine or Activity: _____   **Date:** _____

Colleague: _____

Child(ren)/Age(s): _____

Observation Notes:

Consider the experience from the child(ren)'s point of view. Describe what the child(ren) might have been feeling, thinking, and learning.

How did your colleague help the child(ren) develop good health habits?

Learning Activity D
Recognizing and Reporting the Signs of Child Abuse and Neglect

☐ **Answer** the questions below about the definitions and signs of child abuse and neglect.

☐ **Review** your program's child abuse and neglect reporting procedures. If you need a copy of the procedures, **ask** your director. **Answer** the questions about reporting procedures.

☐ **Read** the reasons why teachers might not report suspected child abuse and neglect. For each reason, **write** a response that explains why signs of possible child abuse and neglect must be reported. An *Answer Sheet* is provided in section 2-10, to serve as an example.

☐ **Share and get feedback** on your responses. **Chart** your feedback in section 2-1.

When you are finished, complete section 2-10, *Reflecting on Your Learning*.

Recognizing Child Abuse and Neglect

What are the four types of child abuse and neglect? Give an example of each type.

Why is it difficult to recognize emotional abuse and neglect?

What causes shaken baby syndrome? How does shaking harm a young child?

Why are teachers in an excellent position to identify signs of possible child abuse and neglect?

How would you describe a typical adult who abuses or neglects children?

State and Local Procedures for Reporting Child Abuse and Neglect

Report to:

_____

(Name)

_____

(Phone)

_____

(Address)

Report must be

☐ Oral   ☐ Written   ☐ Both

Provide this information:

Additional requirements:

Reporting Child Abuse and Neglect

Why I Can't Report	Why I Should Report
Their family problems are none of my business.	
The child's father is out of control. I don't want him to come after me.	
I just started this job, so I don't really know how teachers do things here. Another teacher often yells and belittles children, but I don't want to cause trouble.	
The family might sue me if I report what I've seen and heard.	
I've known this family for years. Their older children were in my group. I know they wouldn't hurt their daughter.	
I don't have any proof, so I can't file a report.	
My supervisor says we should support families. I'll just wait and watch. Things are sure to get better.	

Reflecting on Your Learning

You have now completed all of the learning activities for this module. Whether you are a new or experienced teacher, you have gained new understandings and developed new skills for keeping infants and toddlers healthy. Before going on to the next module, take a few minutes to think about what you have learned. As you complete the steps below, chart your feedback in section 2-1.

☐ **Review the chart** you completed in *Learning Activity A, Using Your Knowledge of Infants and Toddlers to Promote Good Health and Nutrition.* Think about the new ideas you learned as you completed the learning activities in this module. **Add to the chart** examples of things you did while working on this module to keep children healthy.

☐ **Review your responses** to the *Pre-Training Assessment* for this module and **complete** section 2-9b, "Summarizing Progress."

☐ **Explore some curriculum connections.** You will use the skills you developed through module 2, *Healthy,* when implementing a curriculum. Look through your program's curriculum to see how it addresses this topic. For example, *The Creative Curriculum® for Infants & Toddlers* has some sections you might want to review:

- Chapter 9, *Promoting Children's Health,* presents a detailed discussion of health considerations.

- Chapter 9 also includes "Sharing Thoughts About Children's Health," a letter to families in English and Spanish.

☐ **Build partnerships with families.** Share what you learned in this module with the families of children in your care. Here are some ideas:

- Use the development chart in *Learning Activity A* to discuss healthy practices at home.

- Share other information to help families keep their children healthy. For example, you can refer them to the United States Department of Agriculture Web site (www.usda.gov), where they can find information about the dietary guidelines.

- Provide a brief handout based on the bulleted points in *Learning Activity C*, to encourage families to introduce good health and nutrition to their children during daily activities at home.

☐ **Complete the assessments.** Tell the trainer who is guiding you through the modules that you are ready for the knowledge and competency assessments.

☐ **Start a new module.** After completing the assessments successfully, it is time to move on. Congratulations on your progress so far, and good luck with the next module.

Summarizing Progress

Name:_____ **Date:**_____

Did completing this module make you more aware of what you do to promote children's good health? List the strategies you use.

How did you share something you learned with families?

What did you learn about an individual child?

What curriculum connections did you explore?

What do you want to learn more about, and how will you do it?

Creating and Maintaining Indoor and Outdoor Environments That Promote Wellness

Lovette Wipes Her Own Nose

1. What are three things that Ms. Gonzalez did to maintain an environment that promotes wellness?
   - *She opened the window to allow fresh air to circulate.*
   - *She put out more paper towels.*
   - *She placed tissues where children can reach them.*
   - *She assessed children's health when greeting children and their families.*

2. What did Ms. Gonzalez do to prevent germs from spreading?
   - *She helped Lovette blow her nose and throw away the tissue in a waste can with a lid and foot pedal.*
   - *She washed her hands and helped Lovette wash hers.*

Using Daily Routines to Introduce Good Health and Nutrition to Infants and Toddlers

Crunchy Apples and Shiny Teeth

1. What did Mr. Lewis do to help the children develop healthy habits?
   - *He served a healthy snack and modeled eating a healthy food.*
   - *He encouraged the children to help him clear the table.*
   - *He helped children brush their teeth and reminded them to move the brush up and down.*

2. How did the children use self-help skills during daily routines?
   - *Jessica passed a bowl of healthy apple slices.*
   - *They helped clear the table after lunch.*
   - *They brushed their teeth after lunch.*

Recognizing and Reporting Child Abuse and Neglect

Noticing Some Unexplained Bruises

1. What signs of possible child abuse and neglect did Ms. Bates observe?
   - *She has seen unexplained bruises twice.*
   - *She observed a change in the mother's behavior. The mother used to stop and talk, but now she rushes away.*

2. How did the center director support Ms. Bates?
   - *She stayed with Ms. Bates when she called Child Protective Services.*
   - *She reassured Ms. Bates by telling her she met her responsibilities by reporting her suspicions.*

Using Your Knowledge of Young Infants (Birth–8 Months)

Young Infants ...	What I Do to Promote Young Infants' Health and Nutrition
have individual schedules for eating, sleeping, and eliminating	*Individualize daily schedules to meet each infant's need for play, rest, eating, and diapering.*
soil and wet their diapers and clothes	*Change diapers regularly throughout the day. Wash my hands and the infant's when I am finished. Disinfect the changing table after each change.*
get much of their nutrition by breastfeeding or drinking from bottles	*Label bottles with children's names. Refrigerate bottles until used and discard the remains of any bottle from a feeding that is longer than one hour from the beginning of the feeding. Hold infants in my arms when they are drinking and focus my attention on them.*
are developing secure attachments with families and teachers	*Welcome family members to join us during mealtimes. Create a quiet, private space where mothers can nurse. Make mealtimes as family-like as possible, by sitting and talking with children rather than doing chores.*
use their senses (touch, hearing, sight, taste, and smell) to learn about the world	*Wash and disinfect toys and equipment daily. Remove any object that could cause choking.*
have weak neck muscles that cannot immediately support their large, heavy heads	*Support infants' heads with my hand when I lift and carry them. Lift children slowly and steadily, taking care not to let their heads jerk back.*

From *Skill-Building Journal for Caring for Infants & Toddlers, Module 2, Healthy.*
©2005 Teaching Strategies, Inc., Washington, DC 20015, www.TeachingStrategies.com

Using Your Knowledge of Mobile Infants (8–18 Months)

Mobile Infants ...	What I Do to Promote Mobile Infants' Health and Nutrition
pick up small objects by using thumb and forefinger (pincer grasp)	*Offer infants nutritious foods that they can practice picking up and eating by themselves, such as pieces of banana and breadsticks.*
begin to take off hats, shoes, and socks and cooperate when being dressed	*Invite children to participate in dressing as much as they are able and explain how wearing clothes that are appropriate for the weather can help keep them healthy. Step in as necessary to prevent infants from pulling off their hats or shoes on a cold day's walk.*
hold toys, cups, and other objects with two hands	*Offer infants the opportunity to drink milk or juice from plastic cups with lids and handles during snacks and mealtimes.*
crawl and pull themselves up by holding onto furniture and railings	*Provide safe places where children can stretch and exercise by pulling themselves up.*
understand a few words and simple phrases and sometimes follow simple instructions	*Encourage older infants to cough into their elbows. Make up a fun song about how this helps keeps them healthy.*
enjoy water play	*Clean and disinfect water containers and implements daily. Provide fresh water for children to explore.*

From *Skill-Building Journal for Caring for Infants & Toddlers, Module 2, Healthy.*
©2005 Teaching Strategies, Inc., Washington, DC 20015, www.TeachingStrategies.com

Using Your Knowledge of Toddlers (18–36 Months)

Toddlers ...	What I Do to Promote Toddlers' Health and Nutrition
learn self-help skills and use them during routines	*Invite children to participate in daily routines that promote good health, such as dressing to go outdoors and preparing nutritious snacks and meals. Talk about how these activities help people stay healthy.*
gain large motor skills, e.g., running, jumping, kicking, climbing, and throwing	*Provide opportunities throughout the day for toddlers to use large muscles and exercise, both indoors and outdoors. Share children's pleasure in their accomplishment of being upright.*
begin to learn about health and nutrition	*Serve healthy, family-style snacks and/or meals, encouraging toddlers to serve themselves and taste all foods. Join toddlers, to model healthy eating and to guide relaxed conversation.*
may have strong opinions about foods they like and dislike	*Encourage but do not force children to try all foods. Make up songs and stories about children who say* no *but then like new foods when they taste them. Acknowledge that people have different tastes and offer healthy choices.*
begin to gain some bowel and bladder control	*Disinfect bathroom surfaces. Teach children to wash their hands after using the toilet. Wash my hands after helping toddlers use the toilet. Clean up accidents promptly, using surface bleach solution, and wash my hands when done.*
like to do things for themselves, most of the time	*Learn from family members how they involve toddlers in healthy practices at home. Invite, but do not force, children to participate in similar activities in child care.*

2 Healthy

Answer Sheets
Learning Activity D

Recognizing Child Abuse and Neglect

What are the four types of child abuse and neglect? Give an example of each type.

1. *Physical abuse, such as burning a child.*
2. *Sexual abuse, such as photographing a child's genitals.*
3. *Physical neglect, such as failing to get medical attention when a child is sick.*
4. *Emotional abuse or neglect, such as failing to give a baby love and attention.*

Why is it difficult to recognize emotional abuse and neglect?

The signs of emotional maltreatment are rarely physical and some effects do not show up for years. Also, the behaviors of emotionally maltreated and emotionally disturbed children can be similar.

What causes shaken baby syndrome? How does shaking harm a young child?

Shaken baby syndrome is the result of an adult's losing control and violently shaking a young child. Shaking can cause brain and eye hemorrhages and lead to mental retardation, blindness, deafness, and even death.

Why are teachers in an excellent position to identify signs of possible child abuse and neglect?

Teachers see children almost every day. They might detect signs of possible child abuse and neglect that would otherwise go unnoticed.

How would you describe a typical adult who abuses or neglects children?

There is no typical profile of an adult who abuses or neglects children.

Reporting Child Abuse and Neglect

Why I Can't Report	Why I Should Report
Their family problems are none of my business.	*Teachers are mandated reporters who have the right and the responsibility to report suspected child abuse or neglect. My report can protect a child and help a family get needed services.*
The child's father is out of control. I don't want him to come after me.	*An abusive family member might lack the social skills needed to communicate with other people. Discuss your concerns with your director so he or she can support you after you have filed your report.*
I just started this job, so I don't really know how teachers do things here. Another teacher often yells and belittles children, but I don't want to cause trouble.	*Trust your instincts. If you have reason to believe that your colleague's actions are child abuse and neglect, then you should file a report. Parents and other staff may be so used to this person's outbursts that they don't realize children are being harmed.*
The family might sue me if I report what I've seen and heard.	*People who are required by law to report are not responsible for damages if they made the report with good intentions, even if investigators decide that abuse and neglect are not involved. If you are sued, the case will be dismissed when the court learns that you are required by law to file a report.*
I've known this family for years. Their older children were in my group. I know they wouldn't hurt their daughter.	*There is no typical profile of a person who abuses or neglects children. Trust your knowledge of the signs of abuse and neglect. File a report if you suspect that the child is a victim. You will be reporting what you have seen and heard; you will not be accusing anyone.*
I don't have any proof, so I can't file a report.	*You do not need proof to file a report of suspected child abuse or neglect. You must file, if you have seen and heard signs that lead you to suspect abuse or neglect.*
My supervisor says we should support families. I'll just wait and watch. Things are sure to get better.	*While you are watching and waiting, the child continues to be at risk for harm. Until you file your report, the child and family cannot begin receiving the help they need.*

Feedback

You will use this *Feedback Summary* many times as you complete the sections of this module. Feedback is an important part of this training program because it helps you check your understanding, apply knowledge, and build skills. You may seek feedback from your colleagues, your trainer, or members of a child's family. When an *Answer Sheet* is provided, you may also compare your ideas to example answers. Remember that there can be more than one good answer to a question.

This chart lists some feedback sources and provides space for notes. Each time you get feedback, describe, in the appropriate column, how it was provided (e.g., discussing your responses to learning activities, feedback after your interactions with children have been observed, written comments). This will help you remember to get feedback from a variety of sources and in a number of ways.

Section	Source of Feedback				
	Colleague	**Trainer**	**Child's Family**	**Answer Sheet**	**Other**
Overview					
Your Own Responses to the Environment					
Pre-Training Assessment					
A. Using Your Knowledge of Infants and Toddlers to Create a Responsive and Supportive Environment					
B. Creating and Maintaining the Caregiving Environment					
C. Selecting and Displaying Toys and Materials					
D. Planning Daily Routines and a Flexible Schedule					
Reflecting on Your Learning					

Overview

☐ **Answer** the following questions about the three *Overview* stories in module 3 of *Caring for Infants & Toddlers*.

☐ **Compare** your answers to those on the *Answer Sheet* provided in section 3-10.

☐ **Share and get feedback** on your responses. **Chart** your feedback in section 3-1.

When you are finished, read *Your Own Responses to the Environment* in module 3 of *Caring for Infants & Toddlers*.

Creating Indoor and Outdoor Spaces That Support Relationships and Encourage Exploration

It's Time to Get Organized

1. What did Mr. Lewis and Ms. Bates learn by observing the children outdoors?

2. How did Mr. Lewis and Ms. Bates organize the outdoor play area so children can enjoy a variety of active and quiet activities?

Selecting and Arranging Materials and Equipment That Promote Development and Learning

The Wonder of Everyday Materials

1. What did Zora do with the empty food containers?

2. How did Ms. Bates involve Zora's family in the program?

Planning Daily Routines and a Flexible Schedule That Meet Each Child's Needs

Jon and Peter Take a Nap

1. How did Mr. Lewis and Ms. Gonzalez know that Jon and Peter were tired?

2. How did the teachers adapt the planned event to meet individual needs?

**Your Own Responses to the Environment**

☐ **Think** about the way you feel in different environments.

☐ **Answer** the following questions.

☐ **Describe** your favorite place and list three ways you could include features of your favorite place in the infant/toddler environment.

☐ **Share and get feedback** on your responses. **Chart** your feedback in section 3-1.

When you are finished, complete section 3-4, *Pre-Training Assessment.*

Think about a store where you like to shop. What makes it a pleasant place to browse and buy?

Now think about a store you dislike, perhaps a place where you feel frustrated and uncomfortable. What makes it difficult to shop in this store?

Describe your favorite place.

List three ways to include features of your favorite place in the infant/toddler environment.

Pre-Training Assessment

☐ **Read** this list of strategies teachers use to create a responsive and supportive environment for infants and toddlers. Refer to the glossary in *Caring for Infants & Toddlers* if you need definitions of the terms that are used.

☐ **Record** whether you do these things *regularly*, *sometimes*, or *not enough*, by checking the appropriate boxes below.

☐ **Review** your answers.

☐ **List** 3–5 skills you would like to improve or topics you would like to learn more about. (When you finish this module, you will list examples of your new or improved understanding and skills.)

☐ **Share and get feedback** on your responses. **Chart** your feedback in section 3-1.

When you are finished, begin *Learning Activity A, Using Your Knowledge of Infants and Toddlers to Create a Responsive and Supportive Environment*, in module 3 of *Caring for Infants & Toddlers*.

Creating Indoor and Outdoor Spaces That Support Relationships and Encourage Exploration

check the appropriate box — regularly — sometimes — not enough

1. Establish areas for different kinds of play and for diapering, feeding, and other routines. ☐ ☐ ☐

2. Create a relaxed, homelike atmosphere. ☐ ☐ ☐

3. Include open areas where children can safely move and explore. ☐ ☐ ☐

4. Make changes to the environment, if necessary, to support children with disabilities. ☐ ☐ ☐

5. Arrange the outdoor area to support a variety of activities. ☐ ☐ ☐

Selecting and Arranging Equipment and Materials That Promote Development and Learning

check the appropriate box   regularly   sometimes   not enough

6. Provide materials that include the cultures and languages of the children and their families.   ☐ ☐ ☐

7. Provide a variety of open-ended materials that can be used safely in different ways.   ☐ ☐ ☐

8. Offer materials that encourage children to use their senses.   ☐ ☐ ☐

9. Arrange play materials so children can find and return them on their own.   ☐ ☐ ☐

10. Display materials so children can choose them without being overwhelmed or frustrated.   ☐ ☐ ☐

Planning Daily Routines and a Flexible Schedule That Meet Each Child's Needs

check the appropriate box   regularly   sometimes   not enough

11. Allow ample time for completing daily routines.   ☐ ☐ ☐

12. Follow a consistent but flexible schedule that can be adapted to respond to individual and group needs.   ☐ ☐ ☐

13. Plan time each day for the children to be outdoors.   ☐ ☐ ☐

14. Help each child relax and feel comfortable at naptime.   ☐ ☐ ☐

15. Communicate often with families about their children.   ☐ ☐ ☐

Skills to Improve or Topics to Learn More About

☐ **Read the following chart** that lists some typical characteristics of young infants, mobile infants, and toddlers that are important to consider when you are creating a learning environment.

☐ **Write** examples of things you do to create an environment that corresponds to these characteristics. You might describe how you arrange furniture, provide toys and materials, handle routines, interact with infants and toddlers, and partner with families. If you need help getting started, turn to the completed chart in section 3-10.

☐ **Share and get feedback** on your responses. **Chart** your feedback in section 3-1.

☐ **Add** more examples to the chart as you complete the rest of the learning activities in this module and learn more about creating a responsive and supportive environment.

When you are finished, begin *Learning Activity B, Creating and Maintaining the Caregiving Environment*, in module 3 of *Caring for Infants & Toddlers*.

3
Learning Environment

Learning Activity A, continued
Using Your Knowledge of Infants and Toddlers to
Create a Responsive and Supportive Environment

SECTION **3-5b**

Using Your Knowledge of Young Infants (Birth–8 Months)

Young Infants ...	What I Do to Create an Environment for Young Infants
feel most secure at home with their families	*Add homelike touches to make the environment welcoming. Include plants, tapes of families' favorite music, and family photos.*
use all of their senses to learn about the world	
coo, babble, and smile on their own initiative and in response to others	
reach for and pick up objects	
distinguish familiar from unfamiliar things and events	
stretch their legs and kick	
sit, at first using their hands for support and then without support	
begin creeping and crawling	

3 Learning Environment

Learning Activity A, continued
Using Your Knowledge of Infants and Toddlers to
Create a Responsive and Supportive Environment

SECTION **3-5c**

Using Your Knowledge of Mobile Infants (8–18 Months)

Mobile Infants ...	What I Do to Create an Environment for Mobile Infants
creep and then crawl, from one place to another	*Provide open spaces with a variety of surfaces on which to move, e.g., hard floors, soft rugs, grass.*
pull up to standing, cruise by holding furniture or railings, and eventually begin to walk	
sit on the floor or ground and in chairs	
put things in and take them out of containers	
learn about objects by handling them and watching others use them	
sometimes need to get away from the group to be alone or with a special person	
begin simple forms of pretend play	
understand and practice using language	

3 Learning Environment

Learning Activity A, continued
Using Your Knowledge of Infants and Toddlers to
Create a Responsive and Supportive Environment

SECTION **3-5d**

Using Your Knowledge of Toddlers (18–36 Months)

Toddlers ...	What I Do to Create an Environment for Toddlers
walk steadily and smoothly	*Create pathways so toddlers can get easily from place to place without interrupting other children's play or stumbling over obstacles.*
try to throw and catch	
run, jump, and hop	
manipulate objects with hands and fingers and are developing eye-hand coordination	
become increasingly aware of possessions and may struggle with sharing	
make simple decisions	
are learning to use the toilet on their own	
enjoy playing with other children	

☐ **Assess** the indoor and outdoor spaces in which you care for infants and toddlers, using the "Infant/Toddler Environment Checklist" that follows. Rate the items that are relevant to your program. Add additional items in the blank spaces.

☐ **Review** your completed checklist. In the chart that follows the checklist, describe each change you want to make; how you would like to make it; and why it will support children, families, and/or teachers. An example is provided to assist your thinking.

☐ **Read** the example about planning the environment to meet each child's needs.

☐ **Choose** two children in your care with different characteristics, needs, skills, and abilities. **Answer** the questions about each child's family and what the child likes to do. Then **plan** new ways to help each children gain a sense of trust and security and to support their exploration and learning.

☐ **Share and get feedback** on your responses. **Chart** your feedback in section 3-1.

When you are finished, begin *Learning Activity C, Selecting and Displaying Toys and Materials*, in module 3 of *Caring for Infants & Toddlers*.

Infant/Toddler Environment Checklist

Date: _____

Entrance Area

check the appropriate box — we already have this — we could improve this

1.	Displays that welcome and inform families in their home languages and English	☐	☐
2.	Individual, labeled cubbies for children's belongings	☐	☐
3.	Displays of children's creations	☐	☐
4.	A counter for plants, flowers, and/or daily logs	☐	☐
5.	A low bench to sit on while helping children dress or undress	☐	☐
6.	Adult-size chairs	☐	☐
7.	Hooks and storage for adult belongings	☐	☐
8.		☐	☐
9.		☐	☐
10.		☐	☐

Eating Area

check the appropriate box — we already have this — we could improve this

11.	Washable floor	☐	☐
12.	Refrigerator	☐	☐
13.	Microwave	☐	☐
14.	Sink	☐	☐
15.	Counter	☐	☐
16.	Private space and a comfortable chair for nursing	☐	☐
17.	High chairs (2 or 3)	☐	☐
18.	Child-size table and chairs	☐	☐
19.	Cupboards and drawers for storage	☐	☐
20.		☐	☐
21.		☐	☐
22.		☐	☐

Infant/Toddler Environment Checklist, continued

Sleeping Area

check the appropriate box — we already have this — we could improve this

23. Cribs ☐ ☐

24. Cots or mats (for older mobile infants and toddlers) ☐ ☐

25. Comfortable chair ☐ ☐

26. Interesting things to look at (family photos, safety mirrors, mobiles) ☐ ☐

27. Storage for extra sheets and blankets ☐ ☐

28. ☐ ☐

29. ☐ ☐

30. ☐ ☐

Diapering/Toileting Area

check the appropriate box — we already have this — we could improve this

31. Large, sturdy diapering table ☐ ☐

32. Built-in steps or step stool for toddlers ☐ ☐

33. Interesting things to see ☐ ☐

34. Shelf or cupboard for storing supplies ☐ ☐

35. Individual storage containers for children's supplies and extra clothes ☐ ☐

36. Covered trash containers ☐ ☐

37. Child-size sinks ☐ ☐

38. Child-size toilets ☐ ☐

39. Soap, paper towels, trash cans within children's reach ☐ ☐

40. ☐ ☐

41. ☐ ☐

42. ☐ ☐

Infant/Toddler Environment Checklist, continued

Play Area

	check the appropriate box	we already have this	we could improve this
43. Large, open section		☐	☐
44. Small sections where children can spend time alone, in small groups, or with a teacher		☐	☐
45. Low, open shelves used as dividers and to display materials		☐	☐
46. Adult-size chairs		☐	☐
47. Carpeting		☐	☐
48. Mats and protected areas for infants		☐	☐
49. Multiple levels for mobile infants (ramps, carpeted platforms, firm foam cushions)		☐	☐
50. Multiple levels for toddlers (climber with stairs, playhouse, loft)		☐	☐
51. Railings		☐	☐
52. Clear pathways		☐	☐
53. Comfortable chair or sofa		☐	☐
54. Section with washable floor		☐	☐
55. Child-size table and chairs		☐	☐
56. A few simple interest areas for toddlers		☐	☐
57. Items that reflect the unique characteristics of the children (music, posters, family photographs, books)		☐	☐
58.		☐	☐
59.		☐	☐
60.		☐	☐

Infant/Toddler Environment Checklist, continued

Outdoor Play Area

check the appropriate box | we already have this | we could improve this

61. Natural materials (trees, bushes, grass, garden) ☐ ☐

62. Shady areas (trees or shelters) ☐ ☐

63. Different levels and textures (small hills, ramps, flat areas, low climbers with platforms) ☐ ☐

64. Grassy open area ☐ ☐

65. Exploration and play opportunities for children with different skills, interests, and abilities ☐ ☐

66. Safe places for infants (away from the traffic of children who crawl and walk) ☐ ☐

67. Small defined areas for activities (e.g., sand and water play) ☐ ☐

68. Lockable storage area ☐ ☐

69. Safe, hard surface for wheeled toys ☐ ☐

70. ☐ ☐

71. ☐ ☐

72. ☐ ☐

Learning Activity B, continued
Creating and Maintaining the Caregiving Environment

Changing My Infant/Toddler Environment

Change I Want to Make	How I Will Make It	Why It Will Be Supportive
Set up a private, comfortable setting for nursing mothers and infants.	*Move a comfortable chair to a corner of the kitchen area.*	*Mothers and infants can relax while nursing and spending time together.*

Planning the Environment to Meet Each Child's Needs—Example

Child/Age: _Lori, 32 months_   **Date:** _September 2_

What do you know about this child's family life?

Lori has a 6-year-old brother who goes to school. The children live with both parents and their maternal grandparents. Lori is very close to her grandmother. All of the adults in the family work in a family business, a weekly Spanish-language newspaper.

What are some things this child likes to do?

Lately, Lori has been naming things in book illustrations and around the room. Last week we read a storybook with a picture of an older woman. She got very excited and said, "Abuelita." Now she wants to read the book again and again.

Lori likes getting out of her wheelchair when she can. For example, she lies on a wedge and plays on the floor with table toys.

Lori enjoys being outdoors. We roll her wheelchair under a shady tree where she can watch the other children.

How can you change the environment to help this child gain a sense of trust and security and to support his or her explorations and learning?

Invite Lori's abuelita to visit the program.

Ask both grandparents for photographs that we can cover with contact paper and post where Lori can see them.

Review our inventory of books and make sure some of them are relevant to the culture and home language of Lori and her family.

Consult with Lori's family and the early intervention specialist about how to adapt the environment so Lori can get involved in a variety of activities. For example, she could use her wedge pillow outdoors as well as indoors.

Planning the Environment to Meet Each Child's Needs

Child/Age:_____ **Date:**_____

What do you know about this child's family life?

What are some things this child likes to do?

How can you change the environment to help this child gain a sense of trust and security and to support his or her explorations and learning?

Learning Activity B, continued
Creating and Maintaining the Caregiving Environment

Planning the Environment to Meet Each Child's Needs

Child/Age:_____ **Date:**_____

What do you know about this child's family life?

What are some things this child likes to do?

How can you change the environment to help this child gain a sense of trust and security and to support his or her explorations and learning?

Learning Activity C
Selecting and Displaying Toys and Materials

☐ **Assess** the toys and materials in your infant/toddler environment and review your recent observation notes about how the children use them.

☐ **Observe** children, if necessary, to collect fresh information about how they use toys and materials.

☐ **Write** examples of toys and materials that meet the listed criteria.

☐ **Share and get feedback** on your responses. **Chart** your feedback in section 3-1.

When you are finished, complete *Learning Activity D, Planning Daily Routines and a Flexible Schedule*, in module 3 of *Caring for Infants & Toddlers*.

Assessing Our Inventory of Toys and Materials

These items are of interest to and developmentally appropriate for the infants and toddlers in our care:
(List one item per age group.)

Young Infants:

Mobile Infants:

Toddlers:

These items relate to children's families, cultures, and home languages:

1.

2.

These items are almost always available:

1.

2.

These items provide variety:

1.

2.

These items can be used in many different ways:

1.

2.

These items help children feel at home:

1.

2.

These items encourage children to... *(List one item per category.)*

use their senses:

build their small muscles:

move and develop their large muscles:

gain language and literacy skills:

pretend and engage in dramatic play:

explore and discover:

Learning Activity D
Planning Daily Routines and a Flexible Schedule

☐ **Write** your schedule on the blank chart that follows.

☐ **Assess** your schedule using the "Daily Schedule Checklist" that follows the first chart.

☐ **Revise** your schedule, if needed, to reflect what you learned in this activity about meeting children's needs. **Record** your revised schedule in the chart that follows the checklist.

☐ **Share and get feedback** by discussing your ideas with colleagues. Together, **decide** whether to try your suggested changes to the daily schedule. **Chart** your feedback.

When you are finished, complete section 3-9, *Reflecting on Your Learning*.

Daily Schedule

Time	What We Usually Do

Daily Schedule Checklist

check the appropriate box | satisfactory | needs improvement

1. Major events occur in the same order each day.	☐	☐
2. There is sufficient time for daily routines.	☐	☐
3. Each infant follows a personal schedule for eating, sleeping, diapering, and playing.	☐	☐
4. There are sufficient opportunities for adults to interact with children one-on-one.	☐	☐
5. Children have opportunities to be alone.	☐	☐
6. Children have opportunities to spend time in small groups of 2–3 children.	☐	☐
7. There is a balance between active and quiet times.	☐	☐
8. There is a balance between child-initiated and adult-led activities.	☐	☐
9. Children go outdoors twice a day.	☐	☐
10. There is sufficient time for transitions.	☐	☐
11. The schedule is followed consistently but flexibly, and it is adapted as needed to respond to individual children.	☐	☐

Revised Daily Schedule

Time	What We Usually Do

Reflecting on Your Learning

You have now completed all of the learning activities for this module. Whether you are a new or experienced teacher, you have gained new understandings and developed new skills for creating a responsive and supportive environment for infants and toddlers. Before going on to the next module, take a few minutes to think about what you have learned. As you complete the steps below, chart your feedback in section 3-1.

☐ **Review the chart** you completed in *Learning Activity A, Using Your Knowledge of Infants and Toddlers to Create a Responsive and Supportive Environment.* Think about the ideas you learned as you completed the learning activities in this module. **Add to the chart** examples of things you did while working on this module to create a responsive and supportive environment for infants and toddlers.

☐ **Review your responses** to the *Pre-Training Assessment* for this module and **complete** section 3-9b, "Summarizing Progress."

☐ **Explore some curriculum connections.** You will use what you learned in module 3, *Learning Environment*, when implementing a curriculum. Look through your program's curriculum to see how it addresses this topic. For example, *The Creative Curriculum® for Infants & Toddlers* has some sections you might want to review:

- Chapter 16, *Playing With Toys*, "Setting the Stage for Toys"
- Chapter 17, *Dabbling in Art*, "Setting the Stage for Art"
- Chapter 18, *Imitating and Pretending*, "Setting the Stage for Imitation and Pretend Play"
- Chapter 19, *Enjoying Stories and Books*, "Setting the Stage for Enjoying Stories and Books"
- Chapter 21, *Exploring Sand and Water*, "Setting the Stage for Exploring Sand and Water"
- Chapter 22, *Having Fun With Music and Movement*, "Setting the Stage for Music and Movement"
- Chapter 23, *Going Outdoors*, "Setting the Stage for Outdoor Play"

☐ **Build partnerships with families.** Share what you learned in this module with the families of the children in your care. Here are some suggestions:

- Use the chart in *Learning Activity A* to discuss the kinds of safe play materials that interest and support infants and toddlers.
- Plan a workshop so families can learn how to make play materials for infants and toddlers by using simple household items.
- Invite families to review the environment and suggest ways to make it comfortable for their children.

☐ **Complete the assessments.** Tell the trainer who is guiding you through the modules that you are ready for the knowledge and competency assessments.

☐ **Start a new module.** After completing the assessments successfully, it is time to move on. Congratulations on your progress so far, and good luck with the next module.

Reflecting on Your Learning

Summarizing Progress

Name:_____ **Date:**_____

Did completing this module help you set up and evaluate a responsive and supportive environment for infants and toddlers? List the strategies you use.

How did you share something you learned with families?

What did you learn about an individual child, and how do you plan to use this information?

What curriculum connections did you explore?

What do you want to learn more about, and how will you do it?

Answer Sheets
Overview

Creating Indoor and Outdoor Spaces That Support Relationships and Encourage Exploration

It's Time to Get Organized

1. What did Mr. Lewis and Ms. Bates learn by observing the children outdoors?
   - *Ms. Bates learned that some children could not get the equipment they wanted to use and became frustrated.*
   - *Mr. Lewis observed that children were getting in each other's way.*

2. How did Mr. Lewis and Ms. Bates organize the outdoor play area so children can enjoy a variety of active and quiet activities?
   - *They organized toys and equipment to make things easy for the children to see and reach.*
   - *They created protected areas for quiet play and other areas for active play.*

Selecting and Arranging Equipment and Materials That Promote Development and Learning

The Wonder of Everyday Materials

1. What did Zora do with the empty food containers?
   - *She had a wonderful time filling the shopping cart with food.*
   - *She strolled around the room with her shopping cart.*

2. How did Ms. Bates involve Zora's family in the program?
   - *She shared a story of how much Zora enjoyed filling the shopping cart.*
   - *She told Zora's mother that replacements were needed and asked if she had any empty egg cartons.*

Planning Daily Routines and a Flexible Schedule That Meet Each Child's Needs

Jon and Peter Take a Nap

1. How did Mr. Lewis and Ms. Gonzalez know that Jon and Peter were tired?
   - *They saw Jon rubbing his eyes.*
   - *They observed that Peter was standing with his jacket half-on and half-off, although he is usually the first to be ready.*

2. How did the teachers adapt the planned event to meet individual needs?
   - *They decided to divide the group.*
   - *While some children took a walk with Mr. Lewis, Ms. Gonzalez helped Jon and Peter take a nap.*

Using Your Knowledge of Young Infants (Birth–8 Months)

Young Infants ...	What I Do to Create an Environment for Young Infants
feel most secure at home with their families	*Add homelike touches to make the environment welcoming. Include plants, tapes of families' favorite music, and family photos.*
use all of their senses to learn about the world	*Offer infants a variety of safe, interesting objects to explore. Take advantage of daily routines to offer infants experiences with different sounds, tastes, and textures.*
coo, babble, and smile on their own initiative and in response to others	*Provide comfortable chairs and a relaxed atmosphere so you can talk with infants throughout the day during routines and experiences. Use words, your tone, and facial expressions to show your interest and pleasure in being with them.*
reach for and pick up objects	*Provide a variety of safe, interesting objects to explore. Rotate familiar items so that children can explore them without being overwhelmed by choices. Observe so that you know when to introduce new items, and offer help as needed.*
distinguish familiar from unfamiliar things and events	*Carry out individualized daily routines. Offer familiar toys and activities during the day. Observe and be available to help children with new toys and activities, as needed.*
stretch their legs and kick	*Provide safe spaces where infants can be on the floor and stretch and kick their legs.*
sit, at first using their hands for support and then without support	*Provide a safe space where young infants can practice sitting without being knocked over by an older child.*
begin creeping and crawling	*Provide open spaces with a variety of surfaces on which to move, e.g., hard floors, soft rugs, grass.*

Using Your Knowledge of Mobile Infants (8–18 Months)

Mobile Infants...	What I Do to Create an Environment for Mobile Infants
creep and then crawl, from one place to another	*Provide open spaces with a variety of surfaces on which to move, e.g., hard floors, soft rugs, grass.*
pull up to standing, cruise by holding furniture or railings, and eventually begin to walk	*Provide railings or low, secured furniture to hold onto. Low platform ramps can be added to provide interesting new places to explore.*
sit on the floor or ground and in chairs	*Provide a variety of manipulative toys for infants to play with while sitting, such as large pegs and peg boards.*
put things in and take them out of containers	*Make fill and dump toys by decorating coffee cans and filling them with items to dump such as small wooden blocks or pop beads.*
learn about objects by handling them and watching others use them	*Provide a variety of materials to handle and opportunities to see how others use them.*
sometimes need to get away from the group to be alone or with a special person	*Set up safe, quiet areas within your sight, such as a cardboard box or corner of the room. Create spaces where an adult and child can spend time together, such as an armchair in a cozy corner.*
begin simple forms of pretend play	*Provide simple, everyday materials such as hats, bags, spoons and pots.*
understand and practice using language	*Create indoors and outdoor space that are just large enough for two or three children to play and begin to communicate with each other. With colleagues, serve as language models for children.*

Using Your Knowledge of Toddlers (18–36 Months)

Toddlers ...	What I Do to Create an Environment for Toddlers
walk steadily and smoothly	*Create pathways so toddlers can get easily from place to place without interrupting other children's play or stumbling over obstacles.*
try to throw and catch	*Provide beach balls and open spaces, indoors and outdoors, where toddlers can practice throwing and catching. Acknowledge toddlers' developing skills.*
run, jump, and hop	*Give toddlers the opportunity to go outdoors each day so they may run and practice jumping and hopping on padded surfaces.*
manipulate objects with hands and fingers and are developing eye-hand coordination	*Provide manipulative materials, such as large pegs and pegboards and beads to string. Invite toddlers to participate in daily routines that offer opportunities to practice small muscle skills, such as dressing and preparing snack.*
become increasingly aware of possessions and may struggle with sharing	*Encourage, but do not expect, sharing. Provide duplicates of favorite toys, to lessen conflicts. Give toddlers a place to store their special things from home.*
make simple decisions	*Arrange the room so toddlers can see into every area and decide where to go next. Arrange toys and materials clearly so toddlers can choose what they want.*
are learning to use the toilet on their own	*Set up the bathroom area so that toddlers can be as independent as possible when using the toilet and sink.*
enjoy playing with other children	*Provide spaces, materials, and equipment that encourage toddlers to play together, such as a wooden rocking boat. Divide the large group, when possible, so toddlers can be together in small groups.*

Feedback

You will use this *Feedback Summary* many times as you complete the sections of this module. Feedback is an important part of this training program because it helps you check your understanding, apply knowledge, and build skills. You may seek feedback from your colleagues, your trainer, or members of a child's family. When an *Answer Sheet* is provided, you may also compare your ideas to example answers. Remember that there can be more than one good answer to a question.

This chart lists some feedback sources and provides space for notes. Each time you get feedback, describe, in the appropriate column, how it was provided (e.g., discussing your responses to learning activities, feedback after your interactions with children have been observed, written comments). This will help you remember to get feedback from a variety of sources and in a number of ways.

Section	Source of Feedback				
	Colleague	**Trainer**	**Child's Family**	**Answer Sheet**	**Other**
Overview					
Taking Care of Your Body					
Pre-Training Assessment					
A. Using Your Knowledge of Infants and Toddlers to Support Physical Development					
B. Creating an Environment That Supports Physical Development					
C. Responding as Infants and Toddlers Use Physical Skills					
D. Supporting Physical Development Throughout the Day					
Reflecting on Your Learning					

4
Physical

Overview

☐ **Answer** the following questions about the three *Overview* stories in module 4 of *Caring for Infants & Toddlers*.

☐ **Compare** your answers to those on the *Answer Sheet* provided in section 4-10.

☐ **Share and get feedback** on your responses. **Chart** your feedback in section 4-1.

When you are finished, read *Taking Care of Your Body* in module 4 of *Caring for Infants & Toddlers*.

Creating Indoor and Outdoor Environments That Invite Infants and Toddlers to Move and Explore

Zora Is on the Move

1. How does the indoor environment invite Zora to move and explore?

2. What did Ms. Bates and Mr. Lewis do to support Zora's physical development?

4 Physical

Overview, continued

Offering Opportunities for Infants and Toddlers to Use Their Muscles

Dancing Toddlers

1. How did Mr. Lewis support the children's physical development?

2. Why did Mr. Lewis dance with the children?

Responding as Infants and Toddlers Practice and Gain New Physical Skills

Jon Rolls Over

1. What did Ms. Bates do to support Jon's physical development?

2. Why did Ms. Bates watch him, rather than step in to help?

Taking Care of Your Body

☐ **Think** about your own fitness, daily movements on the job, and work environment.

☐ **Answer** the following questions.

☐ **Share and get feedback** on your responses. **Chart** your feedback in section 4-1.

When you are finished, complete section 4-4, *Pre-Training Assessment.*

How do you stay fit? Do you walk regularly, take aerobics classes, or play a sport? Do you eat foods that are high in nutrients and low in fat and sugar?

Do you do a lot of bending and lifting each day? How can you prevent back injuries?

What changes to the environment or the schedule could you and your colleagues try in order to prevent back injuries?

☐ **Read** this list of strategies that teachers use to support the physical development of infants and toddlers. Refer to the glossary in *Caring for Infants & Toddlers* if you need definitions of the terms that are used.

☐ **Record** whether you do these things *regularly*, *sometimes*, or *not enough*, by checking the appropriate boxes below.

☐ **Review** your answers.

☐ **List** 3–5 skills you would like to improve or topics you would like to learn more about. (When you finish this module, you will list examples of your new or improved understanding and skills.)

☐ **Share and get feedback** on your responses. **Chart** your feedback in section 4-1.

When you are finished, begin *Learning Activity A, Using Your Knowledge of Infants and Toddlers to Support Physical Development*, in module 4 of *Caring for Infants & Toddlers*.

Creating Indoor and Outdoor Environments That Invite Infants and Toddlers to Move and Explore

check the appropriate box — regularly / sometimes / not enough

1. Use furniture, platforms, and ramps to create multiple levels. ☐ ☐ ☐

2. Provide a variety of surfaces on which children can lie, roll, crawl, walk, and use wheeled toys. ☐ ☐ ☐

3. Offer safe and interesting objects and materials that invite children to explore with their senses. ☐ ☐ ☐

4. Provide toys and materials that invite children to use their hands and fingers, such as squeeze balls, rattles, and pop beads. ☐ ☐ ☐

5. Provide a variety of equipment and materials that invite children to use their arms and legs. ☐ ☐ ☐

Offering Opportunities for Infants and Toddlers to Use Their Muscles

check the appropriate box — regularly / sometimes / not enough

6. Schedule outdoor play twice a day (in full-day programs). ☐ ☐ ☐

7. Provide opportunities for indoor active play during bad weather. ☐ ☐ ☐

8. Provide materials and activities for children with different levels of fine and gross motor skills. ☐ ☐ ☐

9. Invite children to participate in routines so they can develop and use self-help skills. ☐ ☐ ☐

10. Offer music and movement activities so children can move their bodies and become aware of rhythm. ☐ ☐ ☐

Responding as Infants and Toddlers Practice and Gain New Physical Skills

check the appropriate box — regularly / sometimes / not enough

11. Observe, record, and exchange information with families about each child's physical abilities, interests, and needs. ☐ ☐ ☐

12. Share children's pleasure in their new accomplishments. ☐ ☐ ☐

13. Recognize and respect each child's individual rate of development. ☐ ☐ ☐

14. Ensure safety by adapting the environment and teaching practices as children gain new skills. ☐ ☐ ☐

Skills to Improve or Topics to Learn More About

From *Skill-Building Journal for Caring for Infants & Toddlers, Module 4, Physical.*
©2005 Teaching Strategies, Inc., Washington, DC 20015, www.TeachingStrategies.com

☐ **Read** the following charts that list some typical characteristics of young infants, mobile infants, and toddlers that are important to consider when supporting physical development.

☐ **Write** examples of what you do to support physical development that correspond to these characteristics. You might describe how you arrange furniture, provide toys and materials, handle routines, interact with infants and toddlers, and partner with families. If you need help getting started, turn to the completed chart in section 4-10.

☐ **Share and get feedback** on your responses. **Chart** your feedback in section 4-1.

☐ **Add** more examples to the chart as you complete the rest of the learning activities in this module and learn more about supporting physical development.

When you are finished, begin *Learning Activity B, Creating an Environment That Supports Physical Development*, in module 4 of *Caring for Infants & Toddlers*.

Using Your Knowledge of Young Infants (Birth–8 Months)

Young Infants ...	What I Do to Support Young Infants' Physical Development
gain control of their heads (raise and turn their heads from side to side)	*Support infants' heads as I lift, move, and carry them. Hang interesting pictures or mobiles near cribs and diapering tables to encourage them to lift and turn their heads.*
lie on their stomachs, raise their heads, and use their arms to raise their upper bodies	
reach for and grasp toys and other objects	
pick objects up, let them go, and pick them up again	
move objects from one hand to the other; bang objects together	
roll over (from back to stomach and stomach to back)	
sit on a blanket or rug, propped at first and then without external support	

Using Your Knowledge of Mobile Infants (8–18 Months)

Mobile Infants …	What I Do to Support Mobile Infants' Physical Development
feed themselves finger foods; use a spoon; drink from a cup	*Offer finger foods at snacks and meals. Offer sippy cups with lids, even if there are spills. Provide unlidded cups when children seem ready.*
hold and handle toys such as small blocks, shape boxes, and cars and trucks	
make marks with crayons and markers	
creep or crawl from one place to another	
pull themselves up to standing by holding onto furniture, railings, or people	
pick up small objects using a thumb and forefinger (pincer grasp)	
walk steadily, but may still prefer crawling	

Using Your Knowledge of Toddlers (18–36 Months)

Toddlers ...	What I Do to Support Toddlers' Physical Development
walk well; walk on tiptoe; learn to run without falling	*Take toddlers on walks in and around the center. Provide time each day for active movement, such as running, indoors and outdoors.*
pull and push things, such as boxes, chairs, and wheeled toys	
gain large muscle skills, such as throwing, catching, kicking, jumping, and hopping	
gain small muscle skills, such as turning pages, making marks, pouring, opening containers, and using scissors	
grip with thumb and forefinger (pincer grasp) effectively	
begin to coordinate eye and hand movements, e.g., threading beads on laces	
sit on and use their feet to propel riding toys	

☐ **Read** the example observation notes that follow.

☐ **Choose** two children to observe over the next three days.

☐ **Observe** each child several times as he uses physical skills, both indoors and outdoors. **Take** notes during or right after your observations.

☐ **Review** your notes.

☐ **Summarize** what you learned about each child's physical skills and how the environment supports them, by answering the questions that follow.

☐ **Describe** ways the environment can be changed to further encourage both children's physical skills.

☐ **Share and get feedback** on your responses. **Chart** your feedback in section 4-1.

When you are finished, begin *Learning Activity C, Responding as Infants and Toddlers Use Physical Skills*, in module 4 of **Caring for Infants & Toddlers**.

Observing Children as They Use Physical Skills—Example

Observer: *Ms. Gonzalez*　　　　　　　　　　**Date(s):** *March 15–17*

Child #1: *Frank*　　　　　　　　　　　　　**Age:** *12 months*

Observation Notes:

3/15　　*Frank took eight steps. Sat on carpet near bucket of small plastic blocks. Dumped out blocks. Picked one up; dropped it in can. Got up. Walked quickly across room.*

3/16　　*Frank laughed, while walking and pushing box across grass.*

3/17　　*Frank picked up piece of cheese with thumb and forefinger. Ate cheese.*

What large muscle skills is the child working on?

He walks quickly and pushes objects.

What small muscle skills is the child working on?

He can grasp a block and use his pincer grasp to pick things up.

How does the environment support the child's physical development?

There are open spaces where he can move freely, safe things to push, and finger foods to pick up.

Observer: _Ms. Gonzalez_   **Date(s):** _March 15–17_

Child #2: _Jesse_   **Age:** _11 months_

Observation Notes:

3/15   _Jesse sat on floor. Took cover off bucket of blocks. Dumped out blocks. Put blocks back in can, one by one._

3/16   _Jesse held onto chair. Pulled himself up. Walked to table. Stood at table; picked up crayon; scribbled all over paper taped to table._

3/17   _Jesse sat down on grass. Crawled to Mr. Lewis, who was sitting on log reading to Laura. Jesse reached up; grabbed Mr. Lewis; pulled himself up._

What large muscle skills is the child working on?

He pulls himself up and walks, holding onto furniture. He crawls and sits.

What small muscle skills is the child working on?

He can take a cover off a can, grasp small blocks, and scribble with a crayon.

How does the environment support the child's physical development?

There is sturdy furniture, so he can pull himself up and move from place to place. There are toys and materials that encourage him to build and use fine motor skills.

How can the environment be changed to further encourage **both** children's physical skills?

We can offer a greater variety of materials that encourage children to build and to use a wide range of fine motor skills.

We can make sure that the play yard has railings and other supports that children can use to pull themselves up and move from place to place.

Observing Children as They Use Physical Skills

Observer:_____   **Date(s):**_____

Child #1:_____   **Age:**_____

Observation Notes:

What large muscle skills is the child working on?

What small muscle skills is the child working on?

How does the environment support the child's physical development?

Observer: _____

Date(s): _____

Child #2: _____

Age: _____

Observation Notes:

What large muscle skills is the child working on?

What small muscle skills is the child working on?

How does the environment support the child's physical development?

How can the environment be changed to further encourage **both** children's physical skills?

Learning Activity C

Responding as Infants and Toddlers Use Physical Skills

☐ **Read** the following descriptions of infants and toddlers who are using physical skills and **describe** what you might do in response.

☐ **Choose** two children who are of different ages and who have different approaches to physical activities.

☐ **Describe** each child's physical skills and how he or she handles physical challenges.

☐ **Plan** ways to support the children's use of physical skills.

☐ **Try** your plans and report what happened.

☐ **Share and get feedback** on your responses. **Chart** your feedback in section 4-1.

When you are finished, begin *Learning Activity D, Supporting Physical Development Throughout the Day*, in module 4 of *Caring for Infants & Toddlers*.

What Would You Do and Say?

1. Leroy (8 months) likes to hold, shake, and suck on his rattle. When he shakes it harder, he squeals with delight at the louder sound. What might you do and say to respond to Leroy's use of physical skills?

2. Mariah (24 months) likes filling and emptying plastic cups at the water table. When she misses the table and spills water on the floor—which happens often—she says, "Uh-oh!" What might you do and say to respond to Mariah's use of physical skills?

3. Lance (22 months) enjoys stacking small colored blocks, four or five at a time. When he tries to make a taller stack, it falls down and he knocks the blocks all over the floor. What might you do and say to respond to Lance's use of physical skills?

 **Learning Activity C,** continued
Responding as Infants and Toddlers Use Physical Skills

SECTION **4-7b**

Responding to Individual Children's Physical Skills—Example   Date: _March 28_

	Child: Kenny **Age:** 10 months	**Child:** Lucy **Age:** 24 months
How does this child use fine and gross motor skills and handle physical challenges?	Kenny likes to hold his own spoon and scoop up foods such as yogurt. Sometimes he drops the spoon and uses his hands. Lots of food ends up on his bib and feeding tray. He keeps trying to feed himself.	Lucy likes to throw balls into a box on the floor. She always misses, but she picks up the ball and throws it again.
How will you respond to this child's use of physical skills?	I can continue to let him practice feeding himself. To minimize the mess, I can pour a little yogurt into a dish instead of leaving the carton within his reach. Then I can focus on Kenny, instead of worrying about the mess I'll have to clean up.	I can tell her that I notice how she keeps trying. I can get a bigger box or move the box closer to her. I can suggest that she look at the box as she throws the ball.
How did the child react when you responded?	Kenny dipped his spoon into the dish and got some yogurt on it. He lifted it to his mouth without spilling and ate it. I think the open dish makes it easier for him to scoop. He said, "M-m-m," and we both laughed.	Lucy smiled when I said I noticed how she keeps trying. After I moved the box closer, she got a ball in! She grinned, clapped, picked up the ball, and threw it again.
What did you learn from this experience?	Kenny needs time to practice new skills. I can make feeding experiences better for both of us.	Simple changes in the environment can help children be successful.

From *Skill-Building Journal for Caring for Infants & Toddlers, Module 4, Physical.*
©2005 Teaching Strategies, Inc., Washington, DC 20015, www.TeachingStrategies.com

Learning Activity C, continued
Responding as Infants and Toddlers Use Physical Skills

Responding to Individual Children's Physical Skills

Date: _____

	Child: Age:	Child: Age:
How does this child use fine and gross motor skills and handle physical challenges?		
How will you respond to this child's use of physical skills?		
How did the child react when you responded?		
What did you learn from this experience?		

☐ **Read** the following examples. **Think** about the described event, considering it through the eyes of the child and the adult.

☐ **Describe** a routine or play experience during which you supported physical development. **Explain** what the child (or children) did, how you responded, and what happened next.

☐ **Answer** the questions about the experience.

☐ **Share and get feedback** on your responses. **Chart** your feedback in section 4-1.

When you are finished, complete *Reflecting on Your Learning*.

Supporting Physical Development Throughout the Day—Example 1

Event: *Changing Dennis's Diaper*

Child(ren): *Dennis* **Age(s):** *4 months* **Date(s):** *April 6*

What happened?

Dennis was lying on a blanket on the floor. I knelt next to him and said, "Hi Dennis. It's time for a diaper change." I waited while he turned his head to look at me. Then I picked him up, supporting his head with my hand, and carried him to the changing table. I gently laid him down on his back. Dennis touched his hands together over his tummy. I recited the pat-a-cake rhyme and played by touching my hands together, then touching his. Dennis cooed.

Consider the experience through the eyes of the child(ren). Describe what the child(ren) might be feeling, thinking, and learning.

That's Ms. Bates's voice. I like her, and she likes me. I can see her if I turn my head. My head's a little floppy. I'm glad she puts her hand behind it while carrying me. I can touch my hands together. Ms. Bates can do that, too. She touched my hands. It feels nice.

Consider the experience from your perspective. What were you thinking about ways to support physical development?

Dennis is beginning to control his head. I can help him practice by positioning myself at his level, talking to him, and waiting for him to look at me. He is also exploring how his hands move.

How can you continue supporting development of fine and gross motor skills?

I'll play pat-a-cake to encourage him to bring his hands together. He might be ready to hold things, so I'll offer him a rattle to grasp.

Supporting Physical Development Throughout the Day—Example 2

Event: _Taking a Walk_

Child(ren): _Gina, Ron, and Mae_   **Age(s):** _2 years_   **Date(s):** _April 8_

What happened?

Gina, Ron, and Mae got ready to go for a walk with me. After putting on and zipping their jackets, everyone headed outdoors. Gina asked, "Wagon?" I responded, "Okay, we can take the wagon. We'll take turns sitting and pulling." We got the wagon out of the storage shed; then Gina and Mae climbed in. I said, "Ron and I will take the first turn pulling." Ron said, "Me push." He walked to the back of the wagon and grabbed the edge. I grasped the handle and started walking. Ron pushed from the rear. When we went under a tree, Mae reached up to touch the leaves.

Consider the experience through the eyes of the child(ren). Describe what the child(ren) might be feeling, thinking, and learning.

Gina: "I like riding in the wagon. It feels good to be pulled along."
Ron: "I feel strong when I push the heavy wagon. I can make the wagon move."
Mae: "The leaves are high, but I can stretch to reach them."

Consider the experience from your perspective. What were you thinking about ways to support physical development?

Gina likes riding better than walking. After a while, I'll encourage her to walk and help pull the wagon.

Ron has a lot of self-confidence. He believes he is strong and can push the wagon, even if it is extra heavy with two children in it. I won't discourage him. If I pull, he can push and feel good about his abilities.

Mae enjoys being outdoors and touching things. When it's her turn to walk, we can stop and pick up leaves to add to our collection.

How can you continue supporting development of fine and gross motor skills?

I can plan activities that encourage Gina to use her large muscle skills to walk, run, climb, kick, and so on. I'll try to get her involved in a simple music and movement activity.

I'll keep an eye on Ron to make sure he stays safe while exploring new physical challenges.

Mae might like to collect pine cones that fall from the tree in the outdoor play area.

Supporting Physical Development Throughout the Day

Event:_____

Child(ren):_____ **Age(s):** _____ **Date(s):** _____

What happened?

Consider the experience through the eyes of the child(ren). Describe what the child(ren) might be feeling, thinking, and learning.

Consider the experience from your perspective. What were you thinking about ways to support physical development?

How can you continue supporting development of fine and gross motor skills?

4 | Physical

Reflecting on Your Learning

You have now completed all of the learning activities for this module. Whether you are a new or experienced teacher, you have gained new understandings and developed new skills for supporting the physical development of infants and toddlers. Before going on to the next module, take a few minutes to think about what you've learned. As you complete the steps below, chart your feedback in section 4-1.

☐ **Review the charts** you completed in *Learning Activity A, Using Your Knowledge of Infants and Toddlers to Support Physical Development*. Think about the new ideas you learned as you completed the learning activities in this module. **Add to the charts** examples of things you did while working on this module to support the physical development of infants and toddlers.

☐ **Review your responses** to the *Pre-Training Assessment* for this module and **complete** section 4-9b, "Summarizing Progress."

☐ **Explore some curriculum connections.** You will use the skills you developed through module 4, *Physical*, when implementing a curriculum. Look through your program's curriculum to see how it addresses this topic. For example *The Creative Curriculum® for Infants & Toddlers* has some sections you might want to review:

- Chapter 15, *Getting Dressed*, presents strategies to make dressing a positive experience for all involved.

- Chapter 23, *Going Outdoors*, includes ideas for supporting large and small muscle skills when going outside.

☐ **Build partnerships with families.** Share what you learned in this module with the families of the children in your care. Here are some suggestions:

- Use the physical development charts in *Learning Activity A* to discuss ways to support physical skills at home.

- Provide a copy of your observation notes so a family knows how their child uses physical skills during the program day.

- Write a brief note to families that explains the suggestions that are presented in **Caring for Infants & Toddlers**, *Learning Activity C*, for responding to the physical skills of infants and toddlers.

- Photograph the children as they use physical skills in routines and during play. Send the photos home for families to keep.

☐ **Complete the assessments.** Tell the trainer who is guiding you through the modules that you are ready for the knowledge and competency assessments.

☐ **Start a new module.** After completing the assessments successfully, it is time to move on. Congratulations on your progress so far, and good luck with the next module.

Reflecting on Your Learning

Summarizing Progress

Name:_____ **Date:**_____

Did completing this module make you more aware of what you do to promote children's physical development? List the strategies you use.

How did you share something you learned with families?

What did you learn about an individual child, and how do you plan to use this information?

What curriculum connections did you explore?

What do you want to learn more about, and how will you do it?

Creating Indoor and Outdoor Environments That Invite Infants and Toddlers to Move and Explore

Zora Is on the Move

1. How does the indoor environment invite Zora to move and explore?
   - *The riding toy gives Zora the chance to use her arms and legs.*
   - *Different levels created with cushions invite Zora to climb and jump.*

2. What did Ms. Bates and Mr. Lewis do to support Zora's physical development?
   - *They described Zora's actions, modeling language and letting her know they were aware of what she was doing.*
   - *They shared their interest in and appreciation of her developing physical skills.*

Offering Opportunities for Infants and Toddlers to Use Their Muscles

Dancing Toddlers

1. How did Mr. Lewis support the children's physical development?
   - *He eliminated hazards by cleaning up with the children before dancing.*
   - *He suggested dancing, an activity that helps children become aware of rhythm and the many ways they can move their bodies.*

2. Why did Mr. Lewis dance with the children?
   - *He wanted to share his pleasure and enjoyment in the activity.*
   - *He wanted to model ways for children to participate.*

Responding as Infants and Toddlers Practice and Gain New Physical Skills

Jon Rolls Over

1. What did Ms. Bates do to support Jon's physical development?
   - *She read his cues and put him on the floor.*
   - *She gave him a safe place and time to explore and move.*

2. Why did Ms. Bates watch him, rather than step in to help?
   - *She knew he was safe and that she was nearby if he needed help.*
   - *She wanted to know whether he can roll over on his own.*

Answer Sheets
Learning Activity A

Using Your Knowledge of Young Infants (Birth–8 Months)

Young Infants . . .	What I Do to Support Young Infants' Physical Development
gain control of their heads (raise and turn their heads from side to side)	*Support infants' heads as I lift, move, and carry them. Hang interesting pictures or mobiles in and near cribs and diapering tables to encourage them to lift and turn their heads.*
lie on their stomachs, raise their heads, and use their arms to raise their upper bodies	*Place infants on firm surfaces, such as a blanket on the floor, where they can practice using their muscles.*
reach for and grasp toys and other objects	*Place a variety of interesting, safe, washable objects within reach so infants can look at and reach for them. Guide infants' hands away gently if they are pulling my hair or glasses and explain, "Be gentle."*
pick objects up, let them go, and pick them up again	*Provide interesting, safe, washable objects so infants can practice picking them up and letting them go. Am patient when spoons and other items end up on the floor during mealtime.*
move objects from one hand to the other; bang objects together	*Call infants' attention to the sounds they make by banging objects together. Sit on the floor and play by offering safe, interesting objects for infants to hold. Watch what happens.*
roll over (from back to stomach and stomach to back)	*Provide a safe space where infants have freedom to practice moving. Am aware of what infants are doing, in case they need assistance.*
sit on a blanket or rug, propped at first and then without external support	*Place children in a safe place where they won't be knocked over. Give children time to sit up, and stay nearby in case they need help.*

From *Skill-Building Journal for Caring for Infants & Toddlers, Module 4, Physical.*
©2005 Teaching Strategies, Inc., Washington, DC 20015, www.TeachingStrategies.com

Using Your Knowledge of Mobile Infants (8–18 Months)

Mobile Infants . . .	What I Do to Support Mobile Infants' Physical Development
feed themselves finger foods; use a spoon; drink from a sippy cup	*Offer finger foods at snacks and meals. Offer sippy cups with lids, even if there are spills. Provide unlidded cups when children seem ready.*
hold and handle toys such as small blocks, shape boxes, and cars and trucks	*Offer small toys that are too large to cause an infant to choke. Step back and see what happens. Have duplicates of favorites to prevent conflicts.*
make marks with crayons and markers	*Tape large pieces of paper to a table top and offer a basket of chunky crayons. Redirect them, if necessary, to keep their marks on the paper. Am ready to redirect crayon tasters.*
creep or crawl from one place to another	*Provide a safe environment where infants can move and explore with little interference from adults. Use cushions and low platforms to encourage infants to crawl and climb.*
pull themselves up to standing by holding onto furniture, railings, or people	*Make sure furniture is steady and has rounded corners. Stay alert in case someone stands up but cannot sit back down. Help infants figure out what to do and let them do it, rather than immediately jump in to help.*
pick up small objects using a thumb and forefinger (pincer grasp)	*Encourage infants to help turn pages in a book, eat finger foods at snacks and meals, and play with nesting toys.*
walk steadily, but may still prefer crawling	*Provide plenty of safe indoor and outdoor spaces in which to crawl and practice walking. Respect children who alternate between crawling and walking, and let them decide when they are ready to stop crawling.*

Using Your Knowledge of Toddlers (18–36 Months)

Toddlers …	What I Do to Support Toddlers' Physical Development
walk well; walk on tiptoe; learn to run without falling	*Take toddlers on walks in and around the center. Provide time each day for active movement, such as running, indoors and outdoors.*
pull and push things, such as boxes, chairs, and wheeled toys	*Provide clear, open areas in which toddlers can have fun and feel competent as they push and pull toys, boxes, and chairs.*
gain large muscle skills, such as throwing, catching, kicking, jumping, and hopping	*Plan daily, indoor and outdoor, large muscle activities, such as jumping, playing ball, and climbing. Participate for my own fun and exercise and to show toddlers that I enjoy and value physical activity.*
gain small muscle skills, such as turning pages, marks, pouring, opening containers, and using scissors	*Provide opportunities for children to use small muscles during daily routines, transitions, and activities. Talk with toddlers about what they are doing, to show that I value their growing competence.*
grip with thumb and forefinger (pincer grasp) effectively	*Offer opportunities that encourage toddlers to practice their pincer grasps, such as helping to turn the pages of the book I am reading aloud and zipping jackets after I connect the bottom.*
begin to coordinate eye and hand movements, e.g., threading beads on laces	*Provide simple puzzles, table toys, house-corner props, and art materials so that toddlers can practice picking up and placing small objects and develop eye-hand coordination. At snacks and meals, offer opportunities for children to serve themselves.*
sit on and use their feet to propel riding toys	*Provide large, open spaces, indoors and outdoors, where children can ride safely. Help as necessary to enforce safety rules.*

5 Cognitive

Feedback

You will use this *Feedback Summary* many times as you complete the sections of this module. Feedback is an important part of this training program because it helps you check your understanding, apply knowledge, and build skills. You may seek feedback from your colleagues, your trainer, or members of a child's family. When an *Answer Sheet* is provided, you may also compare your ideas to example answers. Remember that there can be more than one good answer to a question.

This chart lists some feedback sources and provides space for notes. Each time you get feedback, describe, in the appropriate column, how it was provided (e.g., discussing your responses to learning activities, feedback after your interactions with children have been observed, written comments). This will help you remember to get feedback from a variety of sources and in a number of ways.

Section	Source of Feedback				
	Colleague	**Trainer**	**Child's Family**	**Answer Sheet**	**Other**
Overview					
Your Own Experiences as a Learner					
Pre-Training Assessment					
A. Using Your Knowledge of Infants and Toddlers to Support Cognitive Development					
B. Creating an Environment that Encourages Exploration and Discovery					
C. Supporting Infants' and Toddlers' Thinking Skills During Routines					
D. Encouraging Cognitive Development Throughout the Day					
Reflecting on Your Learning					

Overview

Cognitive

☐ **Answer** the following questions about the three *Overview* stories in module 5 of *Caring for Infants & Toddlers*.

☐ **Compare** your answers to those on the *Answer Sheet* provided in section 5-10.

☐ **Share and get feedback** on your responses. **Chart** your feedback in section 5-1.

When you are finished, read *Your Own Experiences as a Learner*, in module 5 of *Caring for Infants & Toddlers*.

Creating an Environment That Invites Infants and Toddlers to Learn by Using Their Senses and Moving Their Bodies

Jon Uses His Senses to Learn About Beads

1. Why did Ms. Gonzalez decide to help Jon explore the beads?

2. What did Jon learn about the beads by using his senses?

5
Cognitive

Overview, continued

Offering Opportunities for Infants and Toddlers to Explore and Begin to Understand Their World

Luci Explores Her Crackers

1. What did Luci learn about the daily routine of snack time?

2. How did Ms. Bates promote Luci's learning about the world around her?

Interacting With Infants and Toddlers in Ways That Encourage Them to Explore

Peter Takes His Time

1. What was Peter's way of dealing with something new?

2. How did Mr. Lewis encourage Peter's curiosity?

5 Cognitive

Your Own Experiences as a Learner

☐ **Think** about a recent experience when you tried to learn a new skill or gain new understanding, such as when you tried a new sport, took an adult education course, or attended a workshop. Consider what helped and what hindered your learning.

☐ **Answer** the following questions about that learning experience.

☐ **Share and get feedback** on your responses. **Chart** your feedback in section 5-1.

When you are finished, complete section 5-4, *Pre-Training Assessment*.

Describe the recent experience when you were learning something new.

What was challenging about learning something new?

How was the new information or skill presented?

How did you feel during the learning experience?

What made this learning experience successful or unsuccessful?

Pre-Training Assessment

☐ **Read** this list of strategies that teachers use to support the cognitive development of infants and toddlers. Refer to the glossary in *Caring for Infants & Toddlers* if you need definitions of the terms that are used.

☐ **Record** whether you do these things *regularly*, *sometimes*, or *not enough*, by checking the appropriate boxes below.

☐ **Review** your answers.

☐ **List** 3–5 skills you would like to improve or topics you would like to learn more about. (When you finish this module, you will list examples of your new or improved understanding and skills.)

☐ **Share and get feedback** on your responses. **Chart** your feedback in section 5-1.

When you are finished, begin *Learning Activity A, Using Your Knowledge of Infants and Toddlers to Support Cognitive Development*, in module 5 of *Caring for Infants & Toddlers*.

Creating an Environment That Invites Infants and Toddlers to Learn by Using Their Senses and Moving Their Bodies

check the appropriate box — *regularly* / *sometimes* / *not enough*

1. Organize the room to help children develop a sense of order. ☐ ☐ ☐

2. Include a variety of interesting things for children to touch, taste, see, hear, and smell. ☐ ☐ ☐

3. Offer open-ended materials that children can use in different ways according to their skills and interests. ☐ ☐ ☐

4. Provide toys and materials that allow infants and toddlers to begin to understand that their actions cause results. ☐ ☐ ☐

5. Provide places and equipment that encourage infants and toddlers to move their bodies. ☐ ☐ ☐

Offering Opportunities for Infants and Toddlers to Explore and Begin to Understand Their World

check the appropriate box — *regularly* / *sometimes* / *not enough*

6. Invite children to participate in daily routines so they feel competent and learn how things work. ☐ ☐ ☐

7. Take children outdoors and into the neighborhood. ☐ ☐ ☐

8. Create opportunities for children to touch, taste, see, hear, and smell. ☐ ☐ ☐

9. Encourage children to experiment, make discoveries, and think. ☐ ☐ ☐

Interacting With Infants and Toddlers in Ways That Encourage Them to Explore

check the appropriate box — *regularly* / *sometimes* / *not enough*

10. Identify and respond to individual children's interests, needs, and learning styles. ☐ ☐ ☐

11. Talk with children about what they are touching, tasting, seeing, hearing, smelling, and doing. ☐ ☐ ☐

12. Share in children's pleasure and excitement about their explorations, discoveries, and accomplishments. ☐ ☐ ☐

13. Introduce words that describe children's experiences and discoveries. ☐ ☐ ☐

14. Recognize when to let children solve problems on their own and when to offer help. ☐ ☐ ☐

15. Answer children's questions and encourage them to ask more. ☐ ☐ ☐

16. Tell families about their children's use of thinking skills. ☐ ☐ ☐

Skills to Improve or Topics to Learn More About

From *Skill-Building Journal for Caring for Infants & Toddlers, Module 5, Cognitive.*
©2005 Teaching Strategies, Inc., Washington, DC 20015, www.TeachingStrategies.com

☐ **Read the following charts** that list some typical characteristics of young infants, mobile infants, and toddlers that are important to consider when supporting cognitive development.

☐ **Write** examples of things you do to support cognitive development that correspond to these characteristics. You might describe how you arrange furniture, provide toys and materials, handle routines, interact with infants and toddlers, and partner with families. If you need help getting started, turn to the completed chart in section 5-10.

☐ **Share and get feedback** on your responses. **Chart** your feedback in section 5-1.

☐ **Add** more examples to the chart as you complete the rest of the learning activities in this module and learn more about supporting cognitive development.

When you are finished, begin *Learning Activity B, Creating an Environment That Encourages Exploration and Discovery*, in module 5 of *Caring for Infants & Toddlers*.

Using Your Knowledge of Young Infants (Birth–8 Months)

Young Infants ...	What I Do to Support Young Infants' Cognitive Development
use their senses to gather information about people and things	*Take advantage of daily routines to invite infants to explore through their senses. Talk with infants about what they might be seeing, hearing, feeling, and tasting.*
visually follow and respond to objects and faces as they move	
put almost everything they handle in their mouths	
hold and manipulate objects	
explore their bodies and how they move	
vocalize to themselves, people, and toys	
begin to understand that their actions have effects	

Using Your Knowledge of Mobile Infants (8–18 Months)

Mobile Infants ...	What I Do to Support Mobile Infants' Cognitive Development
use their senses and movement to explore the world	*Provide a safe environment with interesting toys and materials and where infants can explore with their senses and move freely. Talk with them about what they are experiencing.*
begin to understand that objects and people exist even when they are out of sight	
begin to remember past experiences and use the information in new situations	
imitate adult actions and language	
make choices between clear alternatives	
begin to solve problems on their own	
use actions and words to communicate	

Using Your Knowledge of Toddlers (18–36 Months)

Toddlers . . .	What I Do to Support Toddlers' Cognitive Development
learn by moving and doing	*Give toddlers time to run, kick and throw balls, and play outdoors every day.*
construct understandings about concepts such as size, shape, and weight	
concentrate for longer periods of time	
sometimes think about actions before performing them	
enjoy and learn through pretending and dramatic play	
often want to do things for themselves	
talk in simple sentences	
experiment to see what will happen as a result of their actions	

From *Skill-Building Journal for Caring for Infants & Toddlers, Module 5, Cognitive.*
©2005 Teaching Strategies, Inc., Washington, DC 20015, www.TeachingStrategies.com

☐ **Read** the example reports of what happened when a teacher introduced a new toy to an infant and to a toddler.

☐ **Select** and **make** a toy for one child or more children in your care. It may be one of the toys introduced in the examples or one of your own choosing.

☐ **Introduce** the toy to the child or children.

☐ **Report** what happened when you introduced the toy. Use the blank form that follows the example.

☐ **Write directions** for making the toy and share them with colleagues and families.

☐ **Share and get feedback** on your responses. **Chart** your feedback in section 5-1.

When you are finished, begin *Learning Activity C, Supporting Infants' and Toddlers' Thinking Skills During Routines*, in module 5 of ***Caring for Infants & Toddlers***.

Making a Toy—Infant Example

Date: _March 10_   **Toy:** _Paper plate face mobile_

Child(ren)/Age(s): _Sally, 4 months_

Describe the toy you made.

> _I drew simple faces on two white paper plates, using a thick black marker. Then I stapled them together so there was a face on each side, attached a string, and hung it over the diapering table._

Describe how the child(ren) might use the toy.

> _I will tap it to make it move, and Sally might turn her head to follow it._

What happened when you introduced the toy?

> _Sally smiled and waved her arms._

How did the toy support cognitive development?

> _Sally can focus her eyes on an object and follow it when it moves. She is attracted to contrasts, especially black against white._

Making a Toy—Toddler Example

Date: _March 10_   **Toy:** _Surprise box_

Child(ren)/Age(s): _Reggie, 32 months_

Describe the toy you made.

> *I put some familiar, interesting objects in a cardboard box; taped it shut; and left a hole in the top large enough for a toddler's arm.*

Describe how the child(ren) might use the toy.

> *Reggie might want to pull the box apart rather than guessing what's inside.*

What happened when you introduced the toy?

> *At first, Reggie did want to peek inside the box. Then he understood the idea of identifying an object by the way it feels. He reached in and felt a ball. "It's a ball," he said. He was very excited and pulled it out to see if he was right.*

How did the toy support cognitive development?

> *Reggie used what he already knew about balls—their size and how they feel—to guess what the mystery object was. He used his language skills to name the objects (the ball and others).*

Making a Toy—Infant

Date: _____   Toy: _____

Child(ren)/Age(s): _____

Describe the toy you made.

Describe how the child(ren) might use the toy.

What happened when you introduced the toy?

How did the toy support cognitive development?

Making a Toy—Toddler

Date: _____   **Toy:** _____

Child(ren)/Age(s): _____

Describe the toy you made.

Describe how the child(ren) might use the toy.

What happened when you introduced the toy?

How did the toy support cognitive development?

5 Cognitive

Learning Activity B, continued

Creating an Environment That Encourages Exploration and Discovery

How to Make _____

For age(s): _____

Materials:

Steps:

Playing with the toy:

☐ **Read** the example that follows about how a teacher used a routine to promote an infant's cognitive development.

☐ **Observe** a colleague and a child during a daily routine. Let your colleagues know beforehand why you will be observing them.

☐ **Take notes** about what happens, during or right after your observation.

☐ **Review** your notes and list five things you and your colleagues can do during the routine to support children's thinking skills.

☐ **Share and get feedback** on your responses. **Chart** your feedback in section 5-1.

When you are finished, begin *Learning Activity D, Encouraging Cognitive Development Throughout the Day*, in module 5 of ***Caring for Infants & Toddlers***.

Supporting Thinking Skills—Example

Routine: _Dressing_   **Date:** _February 7_

Colleague: _Ms. Gonzalez_

Child(ren)/Age(s): _Emma (7 months)_

Observation Notes

> *Ms. Gonzalez lifts Emma from high chair. Says, "Emma you have sweet potatoes all down the front of your shirt and overalls." Carries Emma to diapering table; lays her down. Says, "Let's see what clothes your daddy put in your bag today." Takes out red shirt; holds it where Emma can see it. Says, "This is a nice red shirt, Emma." Points to front of shirt, "Look. There's a teddy." Emma squeals and kicks legs. Ms. G. smiles, says, "Let's get you out of your clothes." Unsnaps overalls. Says, "Did you hear the snaps pop, Emma? Pop. Pop. Pop." Emma gurgles. Ms. G. says, "I guess so."*

List five ways to support thinking skills during this routine.

1. *Take plenty of time when dressing an infant; talk about what we are doing and introduce vocabulary, such as* shirt, red, *and* teddy.

2. *Let infants participate as much as they can. Let mobile infants try to undress and dress themselves (e.g., pull off socks).*

3. *Encourage infants to use all of their senses. Talk about how clothes feel; call attention to sounds, such as those made by snaps and zippers.*

4. *Play peek-a-boo to help infants learn about object permanence (people and things still exist, even when out of sight).*

5. *Talk about concepts (e.g., talk about up and down and off and on, while pulling zippers and pants up and down or when one sock is on and one is off.*

Supporting Thinking Skills

Routine: _____   **Date:** _____

Colleague: _____

Child(ren)/Age(s): _____

Observation Notes

List five ways to support thinking skills during this routine.

1.

2.

3.

4.

5.

Learning Activity D
Encouraging Cognitive Development Throughout the Day

☐ **Read** the examples of an "Activity Plan" and "Activity Review" that follow.

☐ **Plan** an activity for the children in your care. **Record** your ideas on the blank "Activity Plan" form provided.

☐ **Implement** the activity.

☐ **Think** about what happened when you implemented your "Activity Plan." **Record** your thoughts about each activity guideline on the "Activity Review" form.

☐ **Share and get feedback** on your responses. **Chart** your feedback in section 5-1.

When you are finished, complete section 5-9, *Reflecting on Your Learning*.

Activity Plan—Example

Activity: _Painting with water_   **Setting:** _Outdoors_

Dates & Times: _Monday, a.m.; Wednesday, p.m.; Thursday, a.m._

Child(ren)/Age(s): _Troy, James, Cindy, Marie, and other toddlers (2 to 2-1/2 years) in group_

Materials:

> _Short-handled paint brushes (various widths)_
> _Painters' hats_
> _Individual small buckets_
> _Water (from the hose)_

What children can do:

> _Paint the shed with water._
> _Experiment with different brushes._
> _Try different ways to use the brushes._
> _Wear hats and pretend to be painters._

What teachers might do and say:

> _Paint alongside children._
> _Help individual children fill their buckets from the hose._
> _Ask open-ended questions that help toddlers think about where the water goes when it disappears._
> _Invite toddlers to use their imaginations by asking, "What color is your paint?"_
> _Be flexible, if toddlers decide to do something other than planned._

Goals (What children might explore and discover):

> _Concepts: wet and dry, up and down, full and empty_
> _The larger brushes hold more water, so you can paint for a longer time._
> _When the water dries, the strokes disappear._
> _Brushes of different widths make different lines and marks._

Activity Review—Example

Activity Guideline	What Happened
I had clear goals for the activity.	*Cindy asked lots of questions about where the water went when it dried. I talked a lot about concepts: wet/dry, up/down, full/empty. By the third time we painted, Troy and Marie were saying the words as they painted.*
I was ready.	*The first time we did this, the buckets were too small; they didn't hold enough water and were tippy. I should have tried them ahead of time. I got larger buckets for the rest of our painting sessions.*
I chose an appropriate setting for the activity.	*Outdoors was perfect for this activity. It was a warm, sunny day, so it didn't matter when water spilled.*
I scheduled the activity for an appropriate time of day.	*Children were more involved during the morning painting sessions. In the afternoon, children were interested in more active play.*
I offered the activity several times.	*Three children painted at a time. By the end of the week, all interested children had turns, and most had a second or third turn.*
I gave a brief, step-by-step explanation of what to do.	*I did this, but perhaps my explanation wasn't clear enough. Troy kept asking, "Where's the paint?"*
I was willing to change my expectations.	*James and Cindy wandered off to the sandbox, where they mixed sand with the water in their buckets. They had thought of new ways to explore water. Later, I talked with them about their discoveries.*

Activity Plan

Activity: _____   **Setting:** _____

Dates & Times: _____

Child(ren)/Age(s): _____

Materials:

What children can do:

What teachers might do and say:

Goals (What children might explore and discover):

Learning Activity D, continued
Encouraging Cognitive Development Throughout the Day

Activity Review

Activity Guideline	What Happened
I had clear goals for the activity.	
I was ready.	
I chose an appropriate setting for the activity.	
I scheduled the activity for an appropriate time of day.	
I offered the activity several times.	
I gave a brief, step-by-step explanation of what to do.	
I was willing to change my expectations.	

Reflecting on Your Learning

You have now completed all of the learning activities for this module. Whether you are a new or experienced teacher, you have gained new understandings and developed new skills for supporting the cognitive development of infants and toddlers. Before going on to the next module, take a few minutes to think about what you have learned. As you complete the steps below, chart your feedback in section 5-1.

☐ **Review the chart** you completed in *Learning Activity A, Using Your Knowledge of Infants and Toddlers to Support Cognitive Development*. Think about the new ideas you learned as you completed the learning activities in this module. **Add to the chart** examples of things you did while working on this module to help infants and toddlers develop thinking skills.

☐ **Review your responses** to the *Pre-Training Assessment* for this module and complete section 5-9b, "Summarizing Progress."

☐ **Explore some curriculum connections.** You will use the skills you developed through module 5, *Cognitive*, when implementing a curriculum. Look through your program's curriculum to see how it addresses this topic. For example *The Creative Curriculum® for Infants & Toddlers* has some sections you might want to review:

- Chapter 7, *Creating a Welcoming Environment*, includes a section on defining play areas outdoors, as well as a section on adapting the environment for children with special needs.
- Chapter 11, *Hellos and Good-byes*, has a section on helping children gain a sense of control over hellos and goodbyes.
- Chapter 12, *Diapering and Toileting*, includes ideas about how you can help children feel competent as they master the new skill of using the toilet.
- Chapter 15, *Getting Dressed*, discusses ways to use dressing to promote children's sense of competence and independence.
- Chapter 20, *Tasting and Preparing Food*, includes ideas about how to promote children's growing independence during snack and mealtimes.

☐ **Build partnerships with families.** Share what you learned in this module with the families of children in your care. Here are some suggestions:

- Use the development charts in module 5, *Learning Activity A* to discuss appropriate ways for families to encourage their children's thinking skills.
- Hold a "Make a Toy" night, when families can make toys for their children with simple materials that you and your colleagues collect (see **Caring for Infants & Toddlers**, module 5, *Learning Activity B*).
- Write notes to families, sharing stories about how their children use thinking skills.
- Make a poster using photographs and specific examples of what teachers and families can do and say to respond when children use thinking skills.

☐ **Complete the assessments.** Tell the trainer who is guiding you through the modules that you are ready for the knowledge and competency assessments.

☐ **Start a new module.** After completing the assessments successfully, it is time to move on. Congratulations on your progress so far, and good luck with the next module.

Reflecting on Your Learning

Summarizing Progress

Name:_____ **Date:**_____

Did completing this module make you more aware of what you do to promote children's cognitive development? List the strategies you use.

How did you share something you learned with families?

What did you learn about an individual child, and how do you plan to use this information?

What curriculum connections did you explore?

What do you want to learn more about, and how will you do so?

Creating an Environment That Invites Infants and Toddlers to Learn by Using Their Senses and Moving their Bodies

Jon Uses His Senses to Learn About Beads

1. Why did Ms. Gonzalez decide to help Jon explore the beads?
   - *She saw that Jon was interested in the beads.*
   - *She wanted to give Jon a chance to learn by using his senses.*

2. What did Jon learn about the beads by using his senses?
   - *He learned how Ms. Gonzalez's beads look, feel, and sound.*
   - *He saw how he looked wearing the beads.*
   - *He learned the sound and meaning of the word* beads, *by hearing Ms. Gonzalez say it while handling the beads.*

Offering Opportunities for Infants and Toddlers to Explore and Begin to Understand Their World

Luci Explores Her Crackers

1. What did Luci learn about the daily routine of snack time?
   - *She learned how people talk with one another and how to be part of a conversation.*
   - *As she ate it, she learned how a cracker feels, smells, tastes.*

2. How did Ms. Bates promote Luci's learning about the world around her?
   - *She sat and talked with her as Luci ate the cracker.*
   - *She responded to what Luci communicated through her actions.*

Interacting With Infants and Toddlers in Ways That Encourage Them to Explore

Peter Takes His Time

1. What was Peter's way of dealing with something new?
   - *He took time to get used to something new.*
   - *He watched from a distance before he crawled through the tunnel.*

2. How did Mr. Lewis encourage Peter's curiosity?
   - *He rolled the ball to Peter when he saw that Peter was interested in it.*
   - *He respected Peter's reluctance to go into the tunnel and let him observe.*
   - *He used a familiar routine, peek-a-boo, to engage Peter.*

Using Your Knowledge of Young Infants (Birth–8 Months)

Young Infants...	What I Do to Support Young Infants' Cognitive Development
use their senses to gather information about people and things	*Take advantage of daily routines to encourage infants to explore through their senses. Talk with infants about what they are seeing, hearing, feeling, and tasting.*
visually follow and respond to objects and faces as they move	*Spend time with infants, talking with them and holding them. Let them have opportunities to study the face of their special teacher, and give them other interesting things to see.*
put almost everything they handle in their mouths	*Provide safe, soft, washable, colorful toys that infants may suck on. Take special care to pick up small bits of carpet, dust, and other small items that infants might eat.*
hold and manipulate objects	*Provide safe, soft, washable, colorful toys that infants can look at, pick up, and with which they may play.*
explore their bodies and how they move	*Provide safe, open spaces where infants can explore moving in different ways. Talk with them about what they are doing.*
vocalize to themselves, people, and toys	*Talk with infants. Respond to their vocalizations. Observe, in order to decide when to be quiet so infants can experience and enjoy making and listening to different sounds.*
begin to understand that their actions have effects	*Respond to infants' sounds, facial expressions, and movements. Remember that I am more interesting and exciting to an infant than any toy could ever be.*

Using Your Knowledge of Mobile Infants (8–18 Months)

Mobile Infants . . .	What I Do to Support Mobile Infants' Cognitive Development
use their senses and movement to explore the world	*Provide a safe environment with interesting toys and materials and where infants can explore with their senses and move freely. Talk with them about what they are experiencing.*
begin to understand that objects and people exist even when they are out of sight	*Play peek-a-boo games with infants. Hide objects under a blanket; then make them reappear.*
begin to remember past experiences and use the information in new situations	*Exchange information with families about children's experiences. Talk with children about what they do at home, and conduct some similar activities in the program. Include children as partners in daily routines.*
imitate adult actions and language	*Provide simple, everyday props such as hats, bags, and empty food containers. Model behaviors and language that I want infants to learn.*
make choices between clear alternatives	*Create an environment that allows infants to make clear choices and sense order. Display toys clearly on low shelves, not in boxes. Offer clear, manageable, meaningful choices, such as, "Would you like a slice of pear or apple for snack?"*
begin to solve problems on their own	*Give children space and time to solve some problems on their own. Always observe so I am ready to step in and help if necessary. When we solve problems together, talk about aspects of the problem and possible solutions.*
use actions and words to communicate	*Observe and respond to what children are telling me through their actions and words. Talk and read with children. Make simple books together about people and things they know. Learn some expressions in children's home languages.*

Using Your Knowledge of Toddlers (18–36 Months)

Toddlers ...	What I Do to Support Toddlers' Cognitive Development
learn by moving and doing	*Give toddlers time to run, kick and throw balls, and play outdoors every day.*
construct understandings about concepts such as size, shape, and weight	*Give toddlers plenty of opportunities to move and play. Invite toddlers to participate in daily routines. Avoid a lot of direct teaching.*
concentrate for longer periods of time	*Protect toddlers from interruptions—even mine—so they can learn to concentrate.*
sometimes think about actions before performing them	*Arrange the environment so it can help toddlers understand limits, make clear choices, and develop a sense of order.*
enjoy and learn through pretending and dramatic play	*Provide dolls and simple props such as hats, bags, and household objects to encourage toddlers' dramatic play.*
often want to do things for themselves	*Arrange the environment so toddlers can be as independent as possible. Allow enough time for daily routines so children can participate as fully as possible, even if it would be faster for me to do everything myself.*
talk in simple sentences	*Extend and enrich toddlers' language. Help toddlers label objects, ideas, and feelings. Learn to speak a few basic words and phrases in children's home languages.*
experiment to see what will happen as a result of their actions	*Offer toddlers materials and activities, such as dough, water play, and blocks, that will allow them to experiment with cause and effect.*

Feedback

You will use this *Feedback Summary* many times as you complete the sections of this module. Feedback is an important part of this training program because it helps you check your understanding, apply knowledge, and build skills. You may seek feedback from your colleagues, your trainer, or members of a child's family. When an *Answer Sheet* is provided, you may also compare your ideas to example answers. Remember that there can be more than one good answer to a question.

This chart lists some feedback sources and provides space for notes. Each time you get feedback, describe, in the appropriate column, how it was provided (e.g., discussing your responses to learning activities, feedback after your interactions with children have been observed, written comments). This will help you remember to get feedback from a variety of sources and in a number of ways.

Section	Source of Feedback				
	Colleague	**Trainer**	**Child's Family**	**Answer Sheet**	**Other**
Overview					
Your Own Experiences With Communication					
Pre-Training Assessment					
A. Using Your Knowledge of Infants and Toddlers to Promote Communication Skills					
B. Creating an Environment That Invites Infants and Toddlers to Enjoy Sounds, Language, Pictures, and Print					
C. Encouraging the Language Development of Infants and Toddlers					
D. Sharing Books With Infants and Toddlers					
Reflecting on Your Learning					

Overview

Communication

☐ **Answer** the following questions about the three *Overview* stories in module 6 of *Caring for Infants & Toddlers*.

☐ **Compare** your answers to those on the *Answer Sheet* provided in section 6-10.

☐ **Share and get feedback** on your responses. **Chart** your feedback in section 6-1.

When you are finished, read *Your Own Experiences With Communication* in module 6 of *Caring for Infants & Toddlers*.

Creating Places Where Infants and Toddlers Can Enjoy Sounds, Language, Pictures, and Print

Lovette Says, "I Want to Read a Book"

1. How did Ms. Gonzalez respond to what Lovette was telling her?

2. How can Ms. Gonzalez and Lovette's mother work together to promote Lovette's communication skills?

Offering Opportunities for Infants and Toddlers to Explore Sounds, Language, Pictures, and Print

Jessica and Adam Tell a Story

1. How did Mr. Lewis encourage Jessica and Adam to use their language skills?

2. How did Ms. Bates encourage the children to use language and emerging literacy skills?

Encouraging and Responding to Infants' and Toddlers' Efforts to Communicate

Mr. Lewis and Sammy Have a Conversation

1. How did Mr. Lewis encourage Sammy to communicate his thoughts and feelings?

2. How did Mr. Lewis let Sammy know that he was listening to him?

Your Own Experiences With Communication

☐ **Discuss** with a colleague your childhood memories of language and literacy learning at home and at school. Compare your experiences. The first set of questions that follows is provided to guide your discussion. You may use it or questions of your own. You do not need to record your answers.

☐ **Think** about how your early language and literacy experiences affect you today.

☐ **Write** answers to the second set of questions that follows.

☐ **Share and get feedback** on your responses. **Chart** your feedback in section 6-1.

When you are finished, complete section 6-4, *Pre-Training Assessment*.

Memories About Your Early Language and Literacy Learning

What books were read to you in childhood? What books did you read to yourself?

What did you write (letters, stories, reports, poetry, and so on)?

What did you enjoy writing?

How did adults encourage you to read and write? Which of their strategies were most successful?

From *Skill-Building Journal for Caring for Infants & Toddlers, Module 6, Communication*. ©2005 Teaching Strategies, Inc., Washington, DC 20015, www.TeachingStrategies.com

Thinking About Your Early Language and Literacy Learning

How did your early language experiences influence the kind of reader, writer, listener, and speaker you are today?

How well do you communicate? Do you think you are sometimes misunderstood? Why or why not?

How comfortable are you with talking, listening, reading, and writing?

Is there anything you might do to increase your comfort level?

6
Communication

Pre-Training Assessment

☐ **Read** this list of strategies that teachers use to promote the communication skills of infants and toddlers. Refer to the glossary in *Caring for Infants & Toddlers* if you need definitions of the terms that are used.

☐ **Record** whether you do these things *regularly*, *sometimes*, or *not enough*, by checking the appropriate boxes below.

☐ **Review** your answers.

☐ **List** 3–5 skills you would like to improve or topics you would like to learn more about. (When you finish this module, you will list examples of your new or improved understanding and skills.)

☐ **Share and get feedback** on your responses. **Chart** your feedback in section 6-1.

When you are finished, begin *Learning Activity A, Using Your Knowledge of Infants and Toddlers to Promote Communication Skills*, in module 6 of *Caring for Infants & Toddlers*.

Creating Places Where Infants and Toddlers Can Enjoy Sounds, Language, Pictures, and Print

check the appropriate box — regularly / sometimes / not enough

1. Provide pleasant sounds and music when children are likely to listen. ☐ ☐ ☐

2. Include a variety of books that correspond to individual and group skills, interests, languages, cultures, and families. ☐ ☐ ☐

3. Make books about familiar people, objects, and events and share them with children. ☐ ☐ ☐

4. Provide inviting, comfortable, cozy spaces for communicating with one child or a small group. ☐ ☐ ☐

5. Provide toys, materials, and equipment that encourage talking and playing together. ☐ ☐ ☐

6. Share pictures and photographs of familiar objects, events, and people, including children's families. ☐ ☐ ☐

Offering Opportunities for Infants and Toddlers to Explore Sounds, Language, Pictures, and Print

check the appropriate box — regularly / sometimes / not enough

7. Use picture and word labels to show where toys and materials are stored. ☐ ☐ ☐

8. Encourage children to notice sounds in their indoor and outdoor environments. ☐ ☐ ☐

9. Provide a variety of papers and writing tools for children who are ready for them. ☐ ☐ ☐

10. Introduce new and interesting sounds, words, and language patterns. ☐ ☐ ☐

11. Read aloud every day, with individual infants and very small groups of toddlers. ☐ ☐ ☐

12. Encourage families to read aloud. ☐ ☐ ☐

13. Model reading and writing during daily routines. ☐ ☐ ☐

Encouraging and Responding to Infants' and Toddlers' Efforts to Communicate

check the appropriate box — regularly / sometimes / not enough

14. Listen and respond to children's gestures, vocalizations, words, and phrases. ☐ ☐ ☐

15. Talk with children about what they see and experience throughout the day. ☐ ☐ ☐

16. Learn a few important words in families' home languages so that the children know that their home language is important to you. ☐ ☐ ☐

17. Share enjoyment of listening, talking, singing, reading, and writing. ☐ ☐ ☐

18. Make comments and pose questions that encourage children to communicate. ☐ ☐ ☐

Skills to Improve or Topics to Learn More About

Learning Activity A

Using Your Knowledge of Infants and Toddlers to Promote Communication Skills

☐ **Read the following charts** that list some typical characteristics of young infants, mobile infants, and toddlers that are important to consider when promoting communication skills.

☐ **Write** examples of how you promote communication skills in ways that correspond to these characteristics. You might describe how you arrange furniture, provide toys and materials, handle routines, interact with infants and toddlers, and partner with families. If you need help getting started, turn to the completed chart in section 6-10.

☐ **Share and get feedback** on your responses. **Chart** your feedback in section 6-1.

☐ **Add** more examples to the chart as you complete the rest of the learning activities in this module and learn more about promoting communication skills.

When you are finished, begin *Learning Activity B, Creating an Environment That Invites Infants and Toddlers to Enjoy Sounds, Language, Pictures, and Print*, in module 6 of *Caring for Infants & Toddlers.*

Using Your Knowledge of Young Infants (Birth–8 Months)

Young Infants . . .	What I Do to Support Young Infants' Communication Skills
coo, gurgle, and smile, to themselves at first and then back and forth with others	*Respond to infants as if they were talking. Smile and coo back to introduce the give-and-take of conversation. Use routines as opportunities to communicate with infants.*
listen and respond to sounds and voices around them	
enjoy listening to simple stories, songs, and rhymes	
cry, make other sounds, move their bodies, and use facial expressions to communicate	
understand and respond to their names and very simple, familiar requests	
begin babbling; produce the sounds of their home language	
use their senses to explore books	

Using Your Knowledge of Mobile Infants (8–18 Months)

Mobile Infants ...	What I Do to Promote Mobile Infants' Communication Skills
use gestures to communicate, such as shaking their heads and pointing	*Respond to infants' communications so they will know their messages are understood. Model language that expresses what they seem to be communicating, e.g., "You've had enough to eat and want to get down."*
understand and respond to gestures, facial expressions, and changes in vocal tone	
continue babbling to themselves; take turns babbling, talking, and singing with others	
learn to turn pages; may be fascinated with page turning	
begin to understand that objects in pictures represent things in the world	
say a few words that refer to interesting people, objects, and actions	
understand and respond to their own names, a few familiar words, and simple requests	
hold crayons and make marks on paper	

Using Your Knowledge of Toddlers (18–36 Months)

Toddlers ...	What I Do to Promote Toddlers' Communication Skills
increase their receptive and expressive vocabularies rapidly	*Talk to toddlers throughout the day. Describe and explain their actions and those of other people. Name objects, actions, people, and feelings. Read books at listening vocabulary levels, to introduce new words.*
speak in sentences that gradually increase from two to several words in length	
understand and respond to many words, simple directions, and questions	
talk about the present, and, as language and thinking skills grow, begin to talk about the past and future	
enjoy books with rhymes and predictable words and phrases they can anticipate and repeat	
coordinate eye and hand movements and gain small muscle skills	
tell very simple stories, use language in creatively, and begin to express feelings with words	

Learning Activity B
Creating an Environment That Invites Infants and Toddlers to Enjoy Sounds, Language, Pictures, and Print

SECTION **6-6a**

☐ Use the charts that follow to describe *what you do now* to implement the suggested practices for using the environment to encourage language and literacy learning.

☐ **Review** your responses; then note *what else you could do* to implement or improve the practices.

☐ **Share and get feedback** on your responses. **Choose** two or three ideas for you and your colleagues to implement. **Chart** your feedback in section 6-1.

When you are finished, begin *Learning Activity C, Encouraging the Language Development of Infants and Toddlers*, in module 6 of **Caring for Infants & Toddlers**.

Encouraging Language Skills

Suggested Practices	What We Do Now	What Else We Could Do
Set up the environment so that it is comfortable for children.		
Arrange the space so children can spend time with a teacher individually.		
Create a few simple interest areas.		
Include interesting things for children to hear, touch, taste, smell, use, and talk about.		
Display colorful pictures of familiar people and objects at children's eye level.		
Provide play materials that encourage communication and storytelling.		
Provide indoor and outdoor settings for children to play house.		

Encouraging Emerging Literacy Learning

Suggested Practices	What We Do Now	What Else We Could Do
Make sets of picture cards.		
Make books that appeal to the children in the group.		
Create a book area that is soft and comfortable and that has attractive displays and good lighting.		
Put books in other areas.		
Offer writing materials.		
Bring books and writing materials outdoors.		

Learning Activity B, continued
Creating an Environment That Invites Infants and Toddlers to Enjoy Sounds, Language, Pictures, and Print

SECTION **6-6d**

Encouraging Emerging Literacy Learning, continued

Suggested Practices	What We Do Now	What Else We Could Do
Provide props and activities related to favorite stories.		
Include an assortment of toys and materials that support the development of the skills used to write.		
Include materials that give toddlers a casual introduction to the letters of the alphabet.		
Use pictures, signs, labels, and charts to communicate important information.		

☐ **Read** the example notes and interpretation that follow.

☐ **Choose** one infant and one toddler to be the focus of this activity.

☐ **Take notes** for three days about what you say and do to encourage the language development of the two children.

☐ **Review** your notes and think about what the child might have been experiencing and learning. Use your notes to **answer** the question about the child's experience.

☐ **Share and get feedback** on your responses. **Chart** your feedback in section 6-1.

When you are finished, complete *Learning Activity D, Sharing Books With Infants and Toddlers,* in module 6 of **Caring for Infants & Toddlers**.

Encouraging an Infant's Language Development—Example

Child/Age: *Dan (9 months)*   **Date:** *April 11–13*

Day One:

I showed Dan the set of animal pictures that Mr. Lewis made. He tried to eat them! Then he dumped them on the floor. I held up the picture of the cow and said, "Moo." He laughed and grabbed the picture from my hand. He looked at it and gurgled.

Day Two:

Dan was sitting on a mat, babbling to himself and patting the floor. I sat with him and said, "What's up, Dan?" I patted the floor, too. He smiled, and I smiled back. We took turns patting the floor, as though we were drumming. I described it, "The floor is hard and smooth."

Day Three:

When Dan arrived this morning, I took him from his dad's arms. His dad said, "Bye-bye, Dan the Man." I said, "Goodbye, Daddy. Have a good day. See you later." Dan laughed and said, "Da-da-da."

Consider these experiences through the eyes of the child. Use your imagination to describe what the child might have been feeling, thinking, and learning.

He might have liked the sound of the word, "Moo." When we were taking turns patting the floor, perhaps he thought, "It's fun to play with you." He could have been learning about taking turns. I think he felt good, because his daddy loves him and he loves his daddy. His vocalizations are becoming more like words.

Encouraging an Infant's Language Development

Child/Age:_____   **Date:** _____

Day One:

Day Two:

Day Three:

Consider these experiences through the eyes of the child. Use your imagination to describe what the child might have been feeling, thinking, and learning.

Encouraging a Toddler's Language Development

Child/Age:_____   **Date:**_____

Day One:

Day Two:

Day Three:

Consider these experiences through the eyes of the child. Use your imagination to describe what the child might have been feeling, thinking, and learning.

Learning Activity D
Sharing Books With Infants and Toddlers

☐ **Read** the examples that follow about reading with an individual child and with a small group.

☐ **Select** a book to read with a particular child in your care. **Select** another book to read with a small group of toddlers. You may choose books you already have or borrow books from your library.

☐ **Prepare** to read the two books.

☐ **Read** the first book to the individual child and the second with a small group of toddlers.

☐ **Answer** the questions about your reading experiences on the forms that follow the examples.

☐ **Share and get feedback** on your responses. **Chart** your feedback in section 6-1.

When you are finished, complete *Reflecting on Your Learning.*

Reading With an Individual Child—Example

Title/Author: Good Night, Gorilla / Peggy Rathmann   **Date:** June 6

Child/Age: Omar (14 months)

Setting: Indoors, before naptime

Briefly describe this book and why you selected it.

This is a board book with only a few words. It's about a zookeeper who says goodnight to all of the animals. I chose it for several reasons: Omar recently went to the zoo with his family and is fascinated by zoo animals; the pictures are very colorful and engaging; and it has a simple, repetitive phrase that Omar can repeat. He is just starting to talk, and his mom told us that he says, "Goodnight," at bedtime.

How did you prepare for reading this book?

I read it and looked closely at the pictures. I noticed quite a few details in the illustrations that I can point out to Omar.

What happened when you read this book?

Omar was very excited. He held the book and turned the pages while I read. Sometimes he pointed to the animals when I said, "Where's the . . . ?" He listened when I pointed out details such as the mouse carrying a banana on every page. By the time we got close to the end, he was pointing to the mouse, himself, and joining in, "Goodnight."

What did you learn about this child?

When a book is just right for Omar, he really enjoys reading. He can hold a book and turn pages. Upon request, he can point to things in pictures.

Reading With a Small Group of Toddlers—Example

Title/Author: Let's Go Visiting / Sue Williams   **Date:** June 6

Children/Ages: Charles, Andrew, and Loni (all are almost 3 years old)

Setting: Outdoors, under a tree

Briefly describe this book and why you selected it.

This book is about a visit to a farm with baby animals. Two phrases are repeated ("Let's go visiting" and "What do you say?"), so the children can join in. There are colors and the numerals 1–6, so children can identify colors and count the animals on each page if they want to. The illustrations are simple, large, colorful, and realistic. The older toddlers are going to visit a farm next week, so this will set the stage.

How did you prepare for reading this book?

I read it and looked closely at the pictures; thought of questions that might involve the children; carried a basket of rubber farm animals outdoors; and brought some photographs of my dog, a golden retriever like the one in the book.

What happened when you read this book?

Andrew sat in my lap; Loni and Charles sat next to me. Andrew held the book out so everyone could see. The children responded to my prompt, "What do you say?", with animal sounds. Charles counted the animals after I read the text. The others talked about what they saw in the pictures and matched the pictures to our rubber farm animals. They were excited to see photographs of my dog. Loni asked, "Will we see ducklings and piglets at the farm?" We also talked about the names of the parents of the baby animals.

What did you learn about these children?

They understand that pictures in books represent real things: our rubber farm animals and the live ones we'll see on our trip. Loni and Andrew know what sounds animals make. Charles is beginning to explore counting. Everyone is excited about our coming trip.

Reading With an Individual Child

Title/Author:_____   **Date:** _____

Child/Age:_____

Setting:_____

Briefly describe this book and why you selected it.

How did you prepare for reading this book?

What happened when you read this book?

What did you learn about this child?

SECTION **6-8d**

Reading With a Small Group of Toddlers

Title/Author:_____   **Date:** _____

Children/Ages:_____

Setting:_____

Briefly describe this book and why you selected it.

How did you prepare for reading this book?

What happened when you read this book?

What did you learn about these children?

Reflecting on Your Learning

You have now completed all of the learning activities for this module. Whether you are a new or experienced teacher, you have gained new understandings and developed new skills for promoting the communication skills of infants and toddlers. Before going on to the next module, take a few minutes to think about what you have learned. As you complete the steps below, chart your feedback in section 6-1.

☐ **Review the chart** you completed in *Learning Activity A, Using Your Knowledge of Infants and Toddlers to Promote Communication Skills.* Think about the new ideas you learned as you completed the learning activities in this module. **Add to the chart** examples of what you did to promote the communication skills of infants and toddlers while working on this module.

☐ **Review your responses** to the *Pre-Training Assessment* for this module and complete section 6-9b, "Summarizing Progress."

☐ **Explore some curriculum connections.** You will use the skills you developed through module 6, *Communication,* when implementing a curriculum. Look through your program's curriculum to see how it addresses this topic. For example, *The Creative Curriculum® for Infants & Toddlers* has some sections you might want to review:

- Chapter 2, *Knowing Infants and Toddlers*, includes the section "Learning About Communicating."

- Chapter 19, *Enjoying Stories and Books*, includes an extensive discussion about introducing books to infants and toddlers.

☐ **Build partnerships with families.** Share what you learned in this module with the families of children in your care. Here are some suggestions:

- Use the development chart in *Learning Activity A* to discuss ways to support children's language and emerging literacy through everyday home experiences.

- Write a one-page handout featuring read-aloud tips from *Learning Activity D.*

- Ask families to share tapes, CDs, rhymes, songs, and stories in their home language, to help children explore language and emerging literacy at the program.

- Suggest that families use sturdy vinyl photo albums to create special books for their children. They can insert photos and pictures that will prompt conversation and learning. Explain that children are likely to chew the pages at first and later may be fascinated with turning the pages. The vinyl pages can be wiped clean. An alternative is to use posterboard and Ziploc® bags. The posterboard can be cut into pages that will fit in the Ziploc® bags.

☐ **Complete the assessments.** Tell the trainer who is guiding you through the modules that you are ready for the knowledge and competency assessments.

☐ **Start a new module.** After completing the assessments successfully, it is time to move on. Congratulations on your progress so far, and good luck with the next module.

Reflecting on Your Learning

Summarizing Progress

Name:_____ **Date:**_____

Did completing this module make you more aware of what you do to promote children's communication skills? List the strategies you use.

How did you share something you learned with families?

What did you learn about an individual child, and how do you plan to use this information?

What curriculum connections did you explore?

What do you want to learn more about, and how will you do it?

Creating Places Where Infants and Toddlers Can Enjoy Sounds, Language, Pictures, and Print

Lovette Says, "I Want to Read a Book"

1. How did Ms. Gonzalez respond to what Lovette was telling her?
   - *She listened to Lovette and looked to see that she was pointing to a particular book.*
   - *She interpreted Lovette's one-word request and waited for Lovette's response.*
   - *She handed the book to Lovette and offered more choices.*
   - *She read rhymes with Lovette.*

2. How can Ms. Gonzalez and Lovette's mother work together to promote Lovette's communication skills?
   - *They can continue to share the new words Lovette uses.*
   - *They can introduce new words with the /b/ sound, such as* bath, bye-bye, *and* baby.
   - *They can let Lovette know that they are excited about her growing language skills. They can respond to her questions and requests, to let her know that they understand what she is saying.*

Offering Opportunities for Infants and Toddlers to Explore Sounds, Language, Pictures, and Print

Jessica and Adam Tell a Story

1. How did Mr. Lewis encourage Jessica and Adam to use their language skills?
   - *He asked Jessica and Adam what they saw on their walk.*
   - *He listened as they answered his question and responded, "That's exciting!"*

2. How did Ms. Bates encourage the children to use language and emerging literacy skills?
   - *She took the children on a walk, to broaden their experiences.*
   - *She provided materials and asked the children if they were writing a story.*
   - *She listened while Jessica and Adam described their stories.*
   - *She shared a book about birds with the children.*

Answer Sheets
Overview, continued

Encouraging and Responding to Infants' and Toddlers' Efforts to Communicate

Mr. Lewis and Sammy Have a Conversation

1. How did Mr. Lewis encourage Sammy to communicate his thoughts and feelings?
    - *He asked Sammy questions and talked with him, although Sammy is too young to use words.*
    - *He noticed Sammy's interest in the mobile and gave him time to watch and respond.*

2. How did Mr. Lewis let Sammy know that he was listening to him?
    - *He took time to follow Sammy's gaze to the mobile.*
    - *He used words to express what he thought Sammy might be communicating.*
    - *He tapped the mobile to make it move, and he talked about it.*
    - *He took Sammy to look at other interesting things.*

Answer Sheets

Learning Activity A

Using Your Knowledge of Young Infants (Birth–8 Months)

Young Infants …	What I Do to Support Young Infants' Communication Skills
coo, gurgle, and smile, to themselves at first and then back and forth with others	*Respond to infants as if they were talking. Smile and coo back to introduce the give-and-take of conversation. Use routines as opportunities to communicate with infants.*
listen and respond to sounds and voices around them	*Play soft music when infants are awake and aware. Point out sounds I hear, even though infants won't understand my language. "Did you hear that airplane fly by? It was noisy."*
enjoy listening to simple stories, songs, and rhymes	*Recite rhymes and sing with infants. Ask their families to share rhymes and songs that infants enjoy at home. Read aloud with infants, especially books with rhyme and repetition.*
cry, make other sounds, move their bodies, and use facial expressions to communicate	*Try to understand infants' messages and respond accordingly. Use words to express what they seem to be saying, e.g., "You are excited to see your daddy." "You like the taste of bananas."*
understand and respond to their names and very simple, familiar requests	*Use an infant's name to get her attention. Ask infants to hand me a toy, hold a shirt, or lift their legs.*
begin babbling; produce the sounds of their home language	*Learn a few words, rhymes, and songs in infants' home languages. Talk with infants as if I understand their babbling, e.g., "Yes, that is a pretty bird. It has a red chest. It's called a robin."*
use their senses to explore books	*Provide cloth and soft vinyl books for very young infants. Securely prop a board book where a very young infant can see it. As infants build small muscle skills, offer board books in chunky and regular formats.*

Using Your Knowledge of Mobile Infants (8–18 Months)

Mobile Infants ...	What I Do to Promote Mobile Infants' Communication Skills
use gestures to communicate, such as shaking their heads and pointing	*Respond to infants' communications so they will know their messages are understood. Model language that expresses what they seem to be communicating, e.g., "You've had enough to eat and want to get down."*
understand and respond to gestures, facial expressions, and changes in vocal tone	*Use smiles and hugs to let infants know that I care about them. Speak in an excited tone of voice to share infants' pleasure in new accomplishments. Use words and gestures to make simple requests.*
continue babbling to themselves; take turns babbling, talking, and singing with others	*Talk and play games that let infants take turns. Pause after talking to give infants time to respond. Invite infants to sing familiar songs.*
learn to turn pages; may be fascinated with page turning	*Provide board books with pages that are easy to turn. Offer catalogs and magazines to infants who love turning pages. Let infants turn pages while reading aloud to them.*
begin to understand that objects in pictures represent things in the world	*Read simple concept and storybooks with pictures of familiar things. Say, "Show me the. . ." or "Where's the . . .?" or "Can you find the . . .?" Invite infants to make sounds that correspond with the pictures, e.g., "Oink"; "Vrroom, vrroom"; "Whoosh."*
say a few words that refer to interesting people, objects, and actions	*Show excitement when infants learn new words. Look at and name things with an infant to introduce new words. For example, point out what I see from the window, "That's a truck. It's on the road."*
understand and respond to their own names, a few familiar words, and simple requests	*Continue using names, speech, and gestures to talk to infants and when giving directions. For example, I hold out my hand while saying, "Luci, please hand me your bowl." Acknowledge infants when they follow directions, "Thank you, Luci."*
hold crayons and make marks on paper	*Introduce chunky crayons and grocery bags or large pieces of paper. Tape paper to the table if it will not stay in place. Demonstrate how to hold the crayon and make marks on paper.*

Using Your Knowledge of Toddlers (18–36 Months)

Toddlers ...	What I Do to Promote Toddlers' Communication Skills
increase their receptive and expressive vocabularies rapidly	*Talk to toddlers throughout the day. Describe and explain their experiences and those of other people. Name objects, actions, people, and feelings. Read books at listening vocabulary levels, to introduce words.*
speak in sentences that gradually increase from two to several words in length	*Restate toddlers' sentences to let them know that I understood them and to model complete language, e.g., "Yes, Kiki is riding a trike."*
understand and respond to many words, simple directions, and questions.	*Have conversations with toddlers so they can learn that it is important to share ideas and feelings with others. Ask questions that let toddlers think and use their skills. Gradually increase the complexity of directions and explanations, as toddlers understand more language.*
talk about the present, and, as language and thinking skills grow, begin to talk about the past and future.	*Invite toddlers to tell stories. Listen patiently so that they have enough time to talk. Ask questions so they can order events (e.g., "What happened next?") and questions that encourage them to make predictions (e.g., "What might happen?").*
enjoy books with rhymes and predictable words and phrases they can anticipate and repeat	*Reread favorite books aloud frequently so toddlers can remember and join in with repetitions. Use phrases from books during routines and activities, e.g., "Mindy, Mindy, what do you see?"*
coordinate eye and hand movements and gain small muscle skills	*Keep crayons and paper on low shelves. Offer finger and easel painting. Provide manipulatives, such as pegs and pegboards, so toddlers can practice using their hands and fingers.*
tell very simple stories, use language creatively, and begin to express feelings with words	*Offer materials for pretend play, such as household items, dress-up clothes, puppets, and small animal and people props. Help toddlers recognize and name feelings and use words to express wants and needs.*

From *Skill-Building Journal for Caring for Infants & Toddlers, Module 6, Communication*.
©2005 Teaching Strategies, Inc., Washington, DC 20015, www.TeachingStrategies.com

Feedback

You will use this *Feedback Summary* many times as you complete the sections of this module. Feedback is an important part of this training program because it helps you check your understanding, apply knowledge, and build skills. You may seek feedback from your colleagues, your trainer, or members of a child's family. When an *Answer Sheet* is provided, you may also compare your ideas to example answers. Remember that there can be more than one good answer to a question.

This chart lists some feedback sources and provides space for notes. Each time you get feedback, describe, in the appropriate column, how it was provided (e.g., discussing your responses to learning activities, feedback after your interactions with children have been observed, written comments). This will help you remember to get feedback from a variety of sources and in a number of ways.

Section	Source of Feedback				
	Colleague	**Trainer**	**Child's Family**	**Answer Sheet**	**Other**
Overview					
Your Own Creativity					
Pre-Training Assessment					
A. Using Your Knowledge of Infants and Toddlers to Encourage Creativity					
B. Supporting Creativity Through Positive Interactions					
C. Encouraging Creative Expression Through Music and Movement					
D. Nurturing Creativity Through Art Experiences					
Reflecting on Your Learning					

7 Creative | Overview

☐ **Answer** the following questions about the three *Overview* stories in module 7 of *Caring for Infants & Toddlers*.

☐ **Compare** your answers to those on the *Answer Sheet* provided in section 7-10.

☐ **Share and get feedback** on your responses. **Chart** your feedback in section 7-1.

When you are finished, read *Your Own Creativity* in module 7 of *Caring for Infants & Toddlers*.

Creating an Environment That Encourages Exploration and Experimentation

Musical Spoons and Pots

1. How did Ms. Bates encourage Jon to explore?

2. How and why did Ms. Bates build on Jon's exploration and experimentation?

Overview, continued

Offering Opportunities for Children to Do Things in Unique Ways

Making Playdough Our Own Way

1. How did Mr. Lewis encourage each child's involvement in making playdough?

2. Why did Mr. Lewis say, "There are several ways to stir."?

Appreciating Each Child's Way of Being Creative

Singing About Peaches

1. How do we know that Ms. Gonzalez has a supportive relationship with Peter?

2. What did Ms. Gonzalez say and do to let Peter know that she values his unique approach to feeding himself?

Your Own Creativity [1]

☐ **Gather** a collection of open-ended materials, such as straws, pipe cleaners, plastic lids, tissue paper, yarn, buttons, and so on. You will also need a timer and writing and drawing tools.

☐ **Choose** a time and place to play with the materials.

☐ **Play** the radio or recorded background music.

☐ **Work** with the open-ended materials for ten minutes. Remember that there is no right or wrong way to use the materials and that you will not be judged or evaluated.

☐ **Reflect** on your exploration of the materials. In the space below, draw or write about what you did and how you felt while you were exploring them.

☐ **Think** about what you learned from this experience and how it applies to encouraging infants' and toddlers' creativity. **Record** your ideas below and **explain** how you will implement them.

☐ **Share and get feedback** on your responses. **Chart** your feedback in section 7-1.

When you are finished, complete section 7-4, *Pre-Training Assessment*.

What materials did you collect? What did you do with them, and how did you feel during the process?

Explain what you learned from this experience that will be useful to you as you encourage infants' and toddlers' creativity. Also explain how you will implement your ideas.

[1] Drew, W. F., Chalufour, I., & Waite-Stupiansky, S. (2003, May). Learning to play again: A constructivist workshop for adults. Beyond the Journal, *Young Children on the Web*. Retrieved April 22, 2005, from http://www.journal.naeyc.org/btj/200305/ConstructWorkshops_Chalufour.pdf

Pre-Training Assessment

☐ **Read** this list of strategies that teachers use to encourage the creativity of infants and toddlers. Refer to the glossary in *Caring for Infants & Toddlers* if you need definitions of the terms that are used.

☐ **Record** whether you do these things *regularly*, *sometimes*, or *not enough*, by checking the appropriate boxes below.

☐ **Review** your answers.

☐ **List** 3–5 skills you would like to improve or topics you would like to learn more about. (When you finish this module, you will list examples of your new or improved knowledge and skills.)

☐ **Share and get feedback** on your responses. **Chart** your feedback in section 7-1.

When you are finished, begin *Learning Activity A, Using Your Knowledge of Infants and Toddlers to Encourage Creativity*, in module 7 of *Caring for Infants & Toddlers*.

Creating an Environment That Encourages Exploration and Experimentation

	check the appropriate box	regularly	sometimes	not enough
1. Create safe, open spaces where infants and toddlers can explore freely.		☐	☐	☐
2. Designate areas with a washable floor and surfaces for messy play and meals.		☐	☐	☐
3. Offer a variety of open-ended materials.		☐	☐	☐
4. Invite children to notice and appreciate interesting and beautiful things.		☐	☐	☐
5. Model creativity by solving problems, being resourceful, and trying new ideas.		☐	☐	☐

Pre-Training Assessment, continued

Offering Opportunities for Children to Do Things in Unique Ways

check the appropriate box — regularly / sometimes / not enough

6. Follow a flexible schedule so children can do things in their own ways and at their own paces. ☐ ☐ ☐

7. Offer messy, open-ended activities such as sand and water play, painting, and making and using playdough. ☐ ☐ ☐

8. Include play materials, props, music, books, and other items that reflect the families, cultures, and ethnicities of all children in the group. ☐ ☐ ☐

9. Encourage sensory exploration during routines and activities. ☐ ☐ ☐

10. Play make-believe games with children. ☐ ☐ ☐

Appreciating Each Child's Way of Being Creative

check the appropriate box — regularly / sometimes / not enough

11. Respond to and build on children's efforts to communicate. ☐ ☐ ☐

12. Get involved in children's play by following and responding to their cues. ☐ ☐ ☐

13. Describe children's use of creative thinking to solve a problem. ☐ ☐ ☐

14. Respect children's concentration. ☐ ☐ ☐

15. Share with families examples of their children's creative thinking and learning. ☐ ☐ ☐

Skills to Improve or Topics to Learn More About

☐ **Read** the example log of children's creativity, to assist your thinking about the children in your care.

☐ **Observe** and **record** examples of infants and toddlers demonstrating the three characteristics of creativity that are listed on the log.

☐ **Plan** ways to share examples of children's creative explorations with families. You might share them through a newsletter, a bulletin board display, a poster, or another format. **Describe** your plan on the form that follows your log.

☐ **Implement** your plan for sharing information with families and **record** some of the families' responses.

☐ **Share and get feedback** on your responses. **Chart** your feedback in section 7-1.

When you are finished, begin *Learning Activity B, Supporting Creativity Through Positive Interactions*, in module 7 of *Caring for Infants & Toddlers*.

Keeping a Log of Children's Creativity—Example

Date(s): _March 20–22_

Infants and toddlers learn through their senses (pay attention to the sight, sound, taste, smell, and feel of things around them).	*Sammy turned his head toward the door when Lovette's father entered the room whistling.*
Infants and toddlers lack inhibition and are eager to experiment and share their ideas.	*Adam put a paper plate on his head and came to show me.*
Infants and toddlers can become absorbed and stay involved in an engaging activity.	*Zora finger painted for ten minutes before washing her hands and moving to another activity.*

Keeping a Log of Children's Creativity

Date(s): _____

Infants and toddlers learn through their senses (pay attention to the sight, sound, taste, smell, and feel of things around them).	
Infants and toddlers lack inhibition and are eager to experiment and share their ideas.	
Infants and toddlers can become absorbed and stay involved in an engaging activity.	

Learning Activity A, continued

Using Your Knowledge of Infants and Toddlers to Encourage Creativity

SECTION **7-5c**

Sharing With Families

How can you share what you observed with families? Describe your plan.

What happened when you implemented your plan? Record some of the comments made by family members.

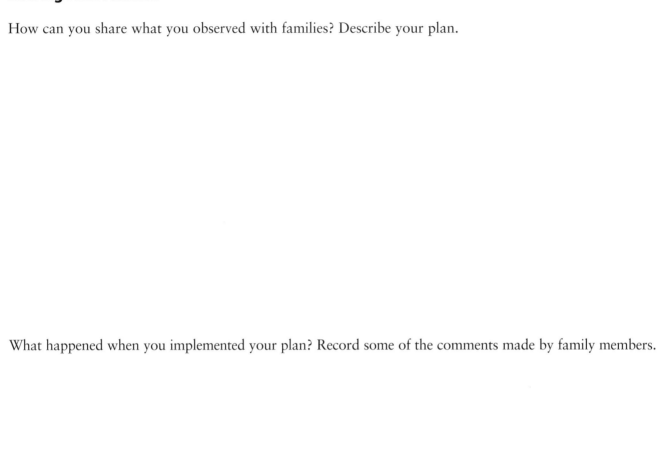

Learning Activity B

Supporting Creativity Through Positive Interactions

☐ **Read** the example provided, to assist your thinking about supporting creativity.

☐ **Use** the list that follows to **rate** how well you and your colleagues support the creativity of infants and toddlers through positive interactions.

☐ **Provide** a brief explanation for your rating and/or indicate changes that you would like to make.

☐ **Share** and get feedback on your responses. **Chart your feedback** in section 7-1.

When you are finished, begin *Learning Activity C, Encouraging Creative Expression Through Music and Movement*, in module 7 of **Caring for Infants & Toddlers**.

Supporting Creativity Through Positive Interactions—Example

check the appropriate box — we do this well / we need to improve

1. We respond to children's attempts to communicate (cries, coos, smiles, gurgles, squeals, eye contact, actions, and/or words).   ☐ ☑

    I marked this "need to improve" because this area is so important. We do build close relationships with the children for whom we have primary responsibility and work hard to get to know them and understand their efforts to communicate. However, we should keep striving to respond even better.

2. We respect toddlers' needs to be independent and to receive reassurance when they need it.   ☑ ☐

    I think that we understand the toddlers in our group. We respect that they are trying hard to be independent, and we know that sometimes leads to frustration. We calmly offer help before children become too frustrated to learn.

Supporting Creativity Through Positive Interactions

1. We respond to children's attempts to communicate (cries, coos, smiles, gurgles, squeals, eye contact, actions, and/or words). ☐ ☐

2. We respect toddlers' needs to be independent and to receive reassurance when they need it. ☐ ☐

3. We also help children build language skills by talking and singing with them throughout the day. ☐ ☐

4. We create opportunities for children to make discoveries. ☐ ☐

5. We encourage sensory exploration (touching, looking, listening, tasting, smelling). ☐ ☐

Supporting Creativity Through Positive Interactions, continued

check the
appropriate box

we do this well

we need to improve

6. We help children focus on cause-and-effect relationships so they can learn about the effects of their actions. ☐ ☐

7. We allow plenty of time and support for children to participate in daily tasks. ☐ ☐

8. We offer children choices. ☐ ☐

☐ **Read** the example of a music and movement activity plan and the description of what happened when it was implemented.

☐ **Plan** a music and movement activity for one or several children.

☐ **Implement** the plan and reflect on what the children did and how you responded.

☐ **Share and get feedback** on your responses. **Chart** your feedback in section 7-1.

When you are finished, complete *Learning Activity D, Nurturing Creativity Through Art Experiences*, in module 7 of *Caring for Infants & Toddlers*.

Encouraging Creative Expression Through Music and Movement—Example

Participant(s): _Children who show interest_   **Date:** _October 9_   **Age(s):** _15–36 months_

Activity: _Exploring the sounds of different kinds of drums_

Describe what you will do.
> *I will bring out our drums. We have homemade drums, tom-toms, bongos, and a floor drum. I will also provide drum sticks of various diameters and lengths. I might play music in the background. I will try to get some CDs from the library featuring drums and drummers.*

Describe what the children can do.
> *Try the different drumsticks with each kind of drum. Try using their hands or sticks to accompany the music. Move and dance while other children drum or while recorded music plays.*

How did you implement the activity?
> *I got everything ready while the children were napping. When they woke up, they could choose to take part in the drum activity. I played the CDs I found at the library.*

How did the children respond?
> *Zora, Ricky, and Jessica came to investigate the drums. Jessica said she wanted the floor drum. I helped her out of her chair, used the wedge pillow so she could sit on the floor, and placed the drum within her reach. Zora and Ricky both wanted the bongos. Ricky took the tom-tom instead. Zora soon lost interest, and Ricky played with the bongos.*

How did this activity encourage creativity?
> *The children made choices: whether to explore the drums, which drum to use, and how to use it. They made discoveries and were introduced to a new kind of music.*

Will you do this activity again? What changes will you make?
> *I will do this again, but next time I will have duplicates of each kind of drum and drumstick.*

Encouraging Creative Expression Through Music and Movement

Participant(s): _____ **Date:** _____ **Age(s):** _____

Activity: _____

Describe what you will do.

Describe what the children can do.

How did you implement the activity?

How did the children respond?

How did this activity encourage creativity?

Will you do this activity again? What changes will you make?

7 Creative

Learning Activity D
Nurturing Creativity Through Art Experiences

☐ **Read** the example of an observation note and an art activity plan.

☐ **Observe** a child exploring art materials over a period of three days and note what the child did and said.

☐ **Review** your observation notes. **Identify** a new art experience that matches this child's skills and interests. Research ideas by using what you learned in this learning activity, books, articles, the Internet, your own files, or by consulting a colleague.

☐ **Implement** the art activity. Then **answer** the questions about the child you observed.

☐ **Share and get feedback** on your responses. **Chart** your feedback in section 7-1.

When you are finished, complete section 7-9, *Reflecting on Your Learning*.

Observation Note—Example

Child: _Zora_   **Age:** _16 months_

Date/Time: _June 7; 10:00 a.m. and 2:00 p.m._

Observer: _Ms. Bates_   **Setting:** _art table_

Art Experiences	What Happened
Day 1 Drawing in sand tray	Zora used her finger to make lines in the sand. Then she picked up a comb and used it to make more lines in the sand.
Tearing and pasting	She chose a handful of paper scraps from the basket. She watched Adam put paste on a scrap, place it on paper, and pat it. Then she put paste on her scrap. The paste got on her hands, and she licked it.

Art Experience Plan—Example

Experience: _Adhesive paper collage_   **Date:** _June 10_

Setting: _Table in art area_   **Number of children at one time:** _2–3_

Where did you find the idea for this activity?

I read about it on the Internet.

Why did you plan this activity?

Zora enjoys exploring with her hands, but I don't think she has the fine motor skills yet for pasting. This activity will encourage her to explore materials without becoming frustrated and without eating paste.

What materials are needed? How did you prepare?

Confetti (purchased and from a paper punch), scraps of yarn and paper, and other colorful items

Adhesive paper (enough to cover a table)

I cut a piece of adhesive paper that was large enough to completely cover the table and with about 3" extra at each end. I took off the backing and secured the paper to the table, with the adhesive side facing up. This created a sticky surface.

I put the basket of the loose materials next to the table where the children could find it.

What did the children do?

The children watched as I placed a few pieces of yarn on the sticky side and patted them so they stayed in place. The children copied me and then stood back to see what they had done. Zora got some yarn from the basket and dropped the pieces on the paper.

What did you do and say to encourage children's creativity?

I described for Zora what she had done, "Look, Zora. You dropped the red yarn on the table. It sticks to the paper." I stepped back to watch what she would do next.

Observation Note

Child: _____   **Age:** _____

Date/Time: _____

Observer: _____   **Setting:** _____

Art Experiences	What Happened
Day 1	
Day 2	
Day 3	

Art Experience Plan

Experience: _____   **Date:** _____

Setting: _____   **Number of children at one time:** _____

Where did you find the idea for this activity?

Why did you plan this activity?

What materials are needed? How did you prepare?

What did the children do?

What did you do and say to encourage children's creativity?

Reflecting on Your Learning

You have now completed all of the learning activities for this module. Whether you are a new or experienced teacher, you have gained new understandings and developed new skills for encouraging the creativity of infants and toddlers. Before going on to the next module, take a few minutes to think about what you have learned. As you complete the steps below, chart your feedback in section 7-1.

☐ **Review** the log you kept in *Learning Activity A, Using Your Knowledge of Infants and Toddlers to Encourage Creativity.* **Add** to the log more examples of the way infants and toddlers demonstrate the three characteristics of creativity.

☐ **Review your responses** to the *Pre-Training Assessment* for this module and **complete** section 7-9b, "Summarizing Progress."

☐ **Explore some curriculum connections.** You will use the skills you developed through module 7, *Creative*, when implementing a curriculum. Look through your program's curriculum to see how it addresses this topic. For example *The Creative Curriculum® for Infants & Toddlers* has some sections you might want to review:

- Part IV, *Putting Quality Into Action: Activities Day by Day*, includes
  - Chapter 17, *Dabbling in Art*
  - Chapter 18, *Imitating and Pretending*
  - Chapter 21, *Exploring Sand and Water*
  - Chapter 22, *Having Fun With Music and Movement*

☐ **Build partnerships with families.** Share what you learned in this module with the families of children in your care. Here are some suggestions:

- Observe and, if possible, photograph children as they explore, investigate, experiment, and try to solve problems. To help families understand the meaning of their children's actions, send home a copy of your observation notes (and photographs) and a brief statement about how the program promotes children's creativity.

- Create and distribute a handout listing the many recyclable items families can collect for the program. Be sure to thank families when they contribute items for the children's use.

- Ask families to share tapes, CDs, rhymes, songs, dances, stories, and art work that will encourage children to explore music, movement, art, and other forms of creative expression at the program.

- Make and distribute a handout that explains how families can support the creativity of their infant or toddler at home. Offer practical suggestions of ways to offer infants and toddlers opportunities to use their senses, make choices and decisions, notice the world around them, listen and move to sounds and music, make sounds and music, and explore art materials.

☐ **Complete the assessments.** Tell the trainer who is guiding you through the modules that you are ready for the knowledge and competency assessments.

☐ **Start a new module.** After completing the assessments successfully, it is time to move on. Congratulations on your progress so far, and good luck with the next module.

7 Creative

Reflecting on Your Learning

Summarizing Progress

Name:_____ **Date:**_____

Did completing this module make you more aware of what you do to encourage the creativity of infants and toddlers? List the strategies you use.

How did you share something you learned with families?

What did you learn about an individual child?

What curriculum connections did you explore?

What do you want to learn more about, and how will you do it?

Creating an Environment That Encourages Exploration and Experimentation

Musical Spoons and Pots
1. How did Ms. Bates encourage Jon to explore?
   - *She made a mobile.*
   - *She hung the mobile over the changing table where he can reach it.*
   - *She told him to listen to the spoons as he touched them.*

2. How and why did Ms. Bates build on Jon's exploration and experimentation?
   - *She showed him how to make music by banging on the pots.*
   - *She knew Jon was interested in making sounds, because of his reaction when the spoons rattled.*

Offering Opportunities for Children to Do Things in Unique Ways

Making Playdough Our Own Way
1. How did Mr. Lewis encourage each child's involvement in making playdough?
   - *He provided materials for the children to explore.*
   - *He invited the children to make the playdough, rather than doing it for them.*

2. Why did Mr. Lewis say, "There are several ways to stir."?
   - *He wanted all of the children to know that he values their curiosity and willingness to try new ways of doing things.*

Appreciating Each Child's Way of Being Creative

Singing About Peaches
1. How do we know that Ms. Gonzalez has a supportive relationship with Peter?
   - *Peter held his arms up, signaling that he wanted Ms. Gonzalez to lift him up.*
   - *Peter seemed to enjoy her singing.*
   - *Ms. Gonzalez showed that she respects Peter by telling him what she was going to do.*

2. What did Ms. Gonzalez do to let Peter know that she values his unique approach to feeding himself?
   - *She gave Peter a spoon of his own.*
   - *She commented on his actions and tried to interpret what they mean.*
   - *She encouraged Peter to feed himself.*

Feedback

You will use this *Feedback Summary* many times as you complete the sections of this module. Feedback is an important part of this training program because it helps you check your understanding, apply knowledge, and build skills. You may seek feedback from your colleagues, your trainer, or members of a child's family. When an *Answer Sheet* is provided, you may also compare your ideas to example answers. Remember that there can be more than one good answer to a question.

This chart lists some feedback sources and provides space for notes. Each time you get feedback, describe, in the appropriate column, how it was provided (e.g., discussing your responses to learning activities, feedback after your interactions with children have been observed, written comments). This will help you remember to get feedback from a variety of sources and in a number of ways.

Section	Source of Feedback				
	Colleague	**Trainer**	**Child's Family**	**Answer Sheet**	**Other**
Overview					
Your Own Sense of Self					
Pre-Training Assessment					
A. Using Your Knowledge of Infants and Toddlers to Foster a Sense of Self					
B. Offering a Program That Promotes Success					
C. Helping Children and Families Cope With Separation					
D. Supporting Toddlers During Toilet Learning					
Reflecting on Your Learning					

Overview

Answer the following questions about the three *Overview* stories in module 8 of *Caring for Infants & Toddlers*.

Compare your answers to those on the *Answer Sheet* provided in section 8-10.

Share and get feedback on your responses. Chart your feedback in section 8-1.

When you are finished, read *Your Own Sense of Self* in module 8 of *Caring for Infants & Toddlers*.

Helping Children Learn About Themselves and Others

Two Firefighters

1. Why did Mr. Lewis tell Lovette that there was another hat on the shelf?

2. How did Mr. Lewis help Lovette and Adam learn about themselves?

Providing Experiences That Allow Children to Be Successful

Zora Can Do It!

1. Why did Ms. Gonzalez watch Zora from a slight distance?

2. Why did Ms. Gonzalez decide to give Zora some help?

Building Supportive Relationships With Individual Children

Luci Loves Yogurt

1. How and why did Ms. Bates use a feeding experience to build a supportive relationship with Luci?

2. What did Ms. Bates do and say to encourage Luci's sense of self?

Your Own Sense of Self

☐ **Think** about your own sense of self and what you base it on.

☐ **Answer** the following questions about your sense of self.

☐ **Share and get feedback** on your responses. **Chart** your feedback in section 8-1.

When you are finished, complete section 8-4, *Pre-Training Assessment.*

When you were young, what behavior did your family and community consider acceptable for children? (For example, were children allowed to be noisy and physically active? Could they look adults directly in the eye when being spoken to? Was it okay for boys to cry or girls to play roughly? Was it acceptable to be smart, athletic, or artistic?)

How and when were you expected to express your ideas and feelings? (For example, were children encouraged to speak up? Was it all right to speak when others were speaking? Did everyone talk at the same time?)

What messages did you receive about your racial or ethnic identity and that of other people? How have those messages influenced your opinions and behavior?

Did you know people with disabilities? (For example, did you attend school with children with disabilities?) What words were used to describe people with disabilities?

How does your sense of self influence your relationships with children? (For example, from where do your expectations for children come? How might your characteristics affect your interactions with children?)

Pre-Training Assessment

☐ **Read** this list of strategies that teachers use to help infants and toddlers build a sense of self. Refer to the glossary in *Caring for Infants & Toddlers* if you need definitions of the terms that are used.

☐ **Record** whether you do these things *regularly*, *sometimes*, or *not enough*, by checking the appropriate boxes below.

☐ **Review** your answers.

☐ **List** 3–5 skills you would like to improve or topics you would like to learn more about. (When you finish this module, you will list examples of your new or improved knowledge and skills.)

☐ **Share and get feedback** on your responses. **Chart** your feedback in section 8-1.

When you are finished, begin *Learning Activity A, Using Your Knowledge of Infants and Toddlers to Foster a Sense of Self*, in module 8 of *Caring for Infants & Toddlers*.

Helping Children Learn About Themselves and Others

check the appropriate box · regularly · sometimes · not enough

1. Include family photos and familiar items that help children feel connected to home while they are at the program. ☐ ☐ ☐

2. Include books, decorations, music, and other items that reflect the cultures of all of the children and teachers. ☐ ☐ ☐

3. Provide multiples of popular play materials so children do not have to share or take turns before they are ready. ☐ ☐ ☐

4. Arrange the furniture, materials, and equipment so mobile infants and toddlers can do things on their own when they are ready. ☐ ☐ ☐

5. Learn and use a few words, songs, and rhymes in the home languages of children whose home language is not English. ☐ ☐ ☐

Providing Experiences That Allow Children to Be Successful

check the appropriate box — regularly / sometimes / not enough

6. Provide a range of activities and materials that can be enjoyed by children with varied skills, abilities, and interests. ☐ ☐ ☐

7. Acknowledge children's efforts as well as their accomplishments. ☐ ☐ ☐

8. Invite children to participate in daily routines to the extent that their abilities and interests allow, even if they take a long time. ☐ ☐ ☐

9. Accept mistakes as a natural part of learning. ☐ ☐ ☐

10. Repeat activities so children can master skills and experience success. ☐ ☐ ☐

Building Supportive Relationships With Individual Children

check the appropriate box — regularly / sometimes / not enough

11. Observe each child regularly to learn about individual needs, skills, abilities, interests, culture, and family experiences. ☐ ☐ ☐

12. Offer verbal and gentle nonverbal contact to show you care about a child's well-being. ☐ ☐ ☐

13. Identify and respond to children's needs and emotions with respect and empathy. ☐ ☐ ☐

14. Help children cope with their feelings about separating from and reuniting with their family members. ☐ ☐ ☐

15. Spend individual time playing, laughing, and talking with each child, every day. ☐ ☐ ☐

Skills to Improve or Topics to Learn More About

☐ **Read the following charts** that list some typical characteristics of young infants, mobile infants, and toddlers that are important to consider when helping children build a sense of self.

☐ **Write** examples of how you help infants and toddlers build a sense of self. You might describe how you arrange your classroom or outdoor area, provide toys and materials, handle routines, interact with children, and partner with families. If you need help getting started, read the completed chart in section 8-10.

☐ **Share and get feedback** on your responses. **Chart** your feedback in section 8-1.

☐ **Add more examples** to the charts as you complete the rest of the learning activities in this module and learn more about helping infants and toddlers build a sense of self.

When you are finished, begin *Learning Activity B, Offering a Program That Promotes Success*, in module 8 of *Caring for Infants & Toddlers*.

Using Your Knowledge of Young Infants (Birth–8 Months)

Young Infants ...	What I Do to Support Young Infants' Physical Development
form strong attachments to family members and teachers	*Get to know individual babies: what they like and don't like, how they respond to different stimuli, and how their families meet their needs at home. Care for a small group of infants over as long a period of time as I can.*
smile and coo on their own initiative and in response to others	
turn their heads and look away when not interested in an activity or toy	
discover and learn to control the movement of their hands and other body parts	
like to be held, cuddled, and amused by simple games and toys	

Learning Activity A, continued

Using Your Knowledge of Infants and Toddlers to Foster a Sense of Self

Using Your Knowledge of Mobile Infants (8–18 Months)

Mobile Infants ...	What I Do to Support Mobile Infants' Physical Development
respond differently to different people they know and may exhibit stranger anxiety	*Limit the number of people who come into the room (other than family members) so infants won't be overwhelmed or scared. Help infants get to know new people at their own paces. Work with colleagues to make sure that each infant has a primary teacher who understands and has a supportive relationship with the child.*
watch people, objects, and activities in their environment	
become attached to favorite items such as stuffed animals or blankets	
move from one place to another by creeping, crawling, or walking	
understand many more words than they can say	

Using Your Knowledge of Toddlers (18–36 Months)

Toddlers ...	What I Do to Support Toddlers' Physical Development
like doing things for themselves most of the time	*Encourage toddlers to take part in routines and to do things for themselves as much as they are able. Provide equipment and materials so they can be independent, such as a sturdy step stool and child-size brooms. Teach toddlers how to do things such as brushing their teeth. Accept that toddlers sometimes want me to do things for them.*
learn to use the toilet on their own	
begin to notice individual characteristics such as gender and skin color	
say *no* when adults ask them to do something	
use words such as *my* and *mine* frequently	

Learning Activity B
Offering a Program That Promotes Success

☐ **Read** the example of how a teacher observed a child and planned ways to promote the child's success.

☐ **Select** one mobile infant and one toddler on whom to focus as you complete this activity.

☐ **Observe** each child for 5–10 minutes, at different times of the day, over the next few days. **Take notes** about what you observe.

☐ **Review** your observation notes and think about what you learned about each child.

☐ **Plan** ways to promote each child's success through the way you structure the environment, routines, and activities and through your interactions. (Make two copies of the planning form.)

☐ **Complete** the form that follows the example. **Describe** the child and **explain** how the program can promote the child's success.

☐ **Share and get feedback** on your responses. **Chart** your feedback in section 8-1.

When you are finished, begin *Learning Activity C, Helping Children and Families Cope With Separation*, in module 8 of *Caring for Infants & Toddlers*.

Offering a Program That Promotes Success—Example

Child: _Janine_ **Age:** _16 months_ **Dates:** _February 6–9_

What Is This Child Like?	How the Program Can Promote Success
What does this child do on arrival? *Her dad usually carries her into the room in the morning. She hangs on tightly and looks around to see who else is in the room. He puts her down, and she stays near him until he leaves. Then she lets me walk her to the rug, where there are toys.*	*Have a toy that she especially likes ready for her when she arrives. Offer her the toy so she finds it easier to get down from her dad's arms. Suggest to her dad that they sometimes hold hands and walk in together, instead of his carrying her.*
What toys and materials does this child enjoy? *She loves things that fit together or inside each other.*	*Play alongside her and introduce some challenges that are within her capabilities.*
What are this child's self-help skills? *She can wipe her face with a washcloth, and she is beginning to use a spoon.*	*Invite her to help prepare food, such as by tearing lettuce and stirring fruit into yogurt.*
What does this child do very well? *Her language skills are really developing. She just started to use single words.*	*Read and talk with her during the day and introduce new words. Model sentences that express the ideas and feelings she communicates with single words and gestures.*

Offering a Program That Promotes Success

Child:_____ **Age:**_____ **Dates:**_____

What Is This Child Like?	How the Program Can Promote Success
What does this child do on arrival?	
What toys and materials does this child enjoy?	
What are this child's self-help skills?	
What does this child do very well?	

Learning Activity C

Helping Children and Families Cope With Separation

☐ **Read** the example of how a teacher helped a child and family cope with separation.

☐ **Choose** a child who has strong feelings about separation to be the focus of this activity.

☐ **Describe** how the child handles separation.

☐ **List** two or more examples of what you do now to support the family and the child, and explain why you do them.

☐ **List** two or more examples of what else you could do to support the family and child, and explain why doing them might help.

☐ **Share and get feedback** on your responses. **Chart** your feedback in section 8-1.

When you are finished, complete *Learning Activity D, Supporting Toddlers During Toilet Learning*, in module 8 of ***Caring for Infants & Toddlers***.

Helping Children and Families Cope With Separation—Example

Child: _Ella_   **Age:** _18 months_   **Date:** _May 4_

How does this child handle separation?

Ella used to bound into our room and quickly find something to do. Now she clings to her mom and begs her to stay. We tell her that her mother has to go to work, and she trusts us, but she is still struggling with her feelings about missing her mom during the day.

	What We Do Now and Why	**What Else We Could Do and Why**
Supporting This Family	1. We ask Ella's mom to allow time in the morning for a little play before she has to leave, so Ella can make a transition from home to the center. 2. We helped her mom establish a goodbye ritual: She kisses Ella's cheeks and says, "Two kisses, and I'm off." This helps Ella say goodbye.	1. We could ask Ella's family to help us make a small album with their photos so Ella can look at it during the day. 2. Describe Ella's day for her mother when she comes to pick Ella up. Also take photos to share with her family. Then her family will know what Ella does during the day.
Supporting This Child	1. We show Ella the picture of her family on the wall and talk about them so she can feel connected to them while she is at the program. 2. We talk about her family during the day, because she does many of the same things with them at home that we do at the center.	1. Continue playing with Ella after her mother leaves, to create a bridge between home and the center. 2. We could read books about topics related to separation, so Ella can understand that her mom will come back to get her.

Helping Children and Families Cope With Separation

Child: _____ Age: _____ Date: _____

How does this child handle separation?

	What We Do Now and Why	**What Else We Could Do and Why**
Supporting This Family		
Supporting This Child		

Learning Activity D
Supporting Toddlers During Toilet Learning

☐ **Read** the example of how a teacher helped a child with toilet learning.

☐ **Select** a child who shows signs of being ready for toilet learning.

☐ **Answer** the questions below about planning support for the child's toilet learning.

☐ **Implement** your toilet learning plan with the child and the child's family.

☐ **Describe** three examples of what happened while you supported the child's toilet learning.

☐ **Share and get feedback** on your responses. **Chart** your feedback in section 8-1.

When you are finished, complete section 8-9, *Reflecting on Your Learning*.

Supporting Toddlers During Toilet Learning—Example

Child: _Jamal_   **Age:** _28 months_   **Dates:** _June 12–26_

What are some of the signs that this child is ready for toilet learning?

He says that he wants to wear underpants like his big brother. He can stay dry for 2–3 hours at a time, and he can dress and undress himself.

Describe your relationship with this child.

I've been Jamal's teacher since he was 10 months old. His previous primary teacher moved away. I think we have a good relationship, and we're used to each other. I appreciate his energy and creative spirit. He is one of the last children to go home, so we often read together at the end of the day. He loves books. Jamal can get frustrated when tasks are too difficult.

What can you do to take advantage of this child's strengths?

We can read books about using the potty. He can hold one of the dolls on the toilet, and we can talk about what the doll is doing. I can remind him to go to the bathroom every two hours or so.

What problems might come up? How will you handle them?

Jamal might get upset when he has an accident. I will be patient and matter-of-fact while helping him change into clean clothes. I'll make sure his family provides plenty of extra clothes, so he won't have to worry about being wet.

How will you and the family work together—before and during toilet learning—to help this child succeed?

Before getting started, I will describe the readiness signs we have seen and ask what they have observed at home. I will ask about their family's preferences related to toilet learning (e.g., what words to use with Jamal and how the family helped his older brother learn to use the toilet). We will discuss our center's approach to toilet learning and agree on a joint plan for Jamal.

During toilet learning, we will talk regularly about Jamal's progress and change our plans if necessary.

Share three examples of what happened as you supported the child's toilet learning. Describe what you and the child did.

1. *Jamal and I read a potty book for boys. He was excited about starting toilet learning.*

2. *This afternoon, Jamal and a friend were so involved in their sandbox play that he forgot about using the toilet and wet his pants. He wasn't upset until I asked him to go inside to change. I told him, "It's okay. I'll help you clean up and get changed." That helped him calm down.*

3. *On Monday, Jamal told me about his weekend. "I stayed dry!" he said. "All day!" I responded, "Wow, Jamal! You are learning to use the toilet like your big brother."*

Supporting Toddlers During Toilet Learning

Child: _____   **Age:** _____   **Dates:** _____

What are some of the signs that this child is ready for toilet learning?

Describe your relationship with this child.

What can you do to take advantage of this child's strengths?

What problems might come up? How will you handle them?

How will you and the family work together—before and during toilet learning—to help this child succeed?

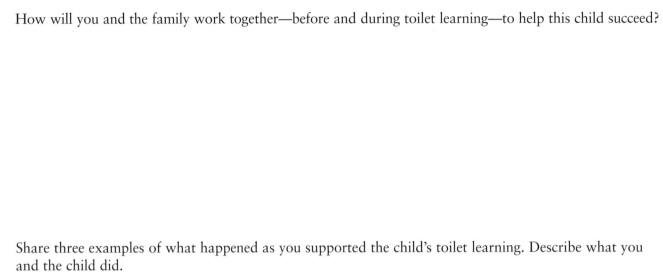

Share three examples of what happened as you supported the child's toilet learning. Describe what you and the child did.

You have now completed all of the learning activities for this module. Whether you are a new or experienced teacher, you have gained new understandings and developed new skills for helping infants and toddlers build a sense of self. As you complete the steps below, chart your feedback in section 8-1.

☐ **Review** the log you kept in *Learning Activity A, Using Your Knowledge of Infants and Toddlers to Foster a Sense of Self*. **Add** to the log more examples of infants and toddlers who are building a sense of self.

☐ **Review your responses** to the *Pre-Training Assessment* for this module and **complete** section 8-9b, "Summarizing Progress."

☐ **Explore some curriculum connections.** You will use the skills you developed through module 8, *Self*, when implementing a curriculum. Look through your program's curriculum to see how it addresses this topic. For example *The Creative Curriculum® for Infants & Toddlers* has some sections you might want to review:

- Chapter 2, *Knowing Infants and Toddlers*, includes discussions about self-concept and emotional development.

- Part III, *Putting Quality Into Action: Routines Day by Day*, explains how to individualize daily routines.

☐ **Build partnerships with families.** Share what you learned in this module with the families of the children in your care. Here are some suggestions:

- Plan and lead a family workshop on ways they can involve their children in routines at home. Make extra handouts and videotape the session so families who cannot attend can still participate and learn.

- Update or create a handout for families about your program's approach to toilet learning. Invite families whose children have already learned to use the toilet while attending the program to review the handout and give their feedback. Address their suggestions before sharing the handout with families.

- Ask the local librarian to help you compile a list of books that can support children who are experiencing separation anxiety. Ask your director to include funds in the budget so you can make family book-packs that include some of the suggested books. The packs can also include a handout of ideas for families to use at home, such as playing peek-a-boo or role-playing separations and reunions.

☐ **Complete the assessments.** Tell the trainer who is guiding you through the modules that you are ready for the knowledge and competency assessments.

☐ **Start a new module.** After completing the assessments successfully, it is time to move on. Congratulations on your progress so far, and good luck with the next module.

Summarizing Progress

Name:_____ **Date:**_____

Did completing this module make you more aware of what you do to help infants and toddlers build a sense of self? List the strategies you use.

How did you share something you learned with families?

What did you learn about an individual child?

What curriculum connections did you explore?

What do you want to learn more about, and how will you do it?

Helping Children Learn About Themselves and Others

Two Firefighters

1. Why did Mr. Lewis tell Lovette that there was another hat on the shelf?
   - *He saw her reach for Adam's hat and heard her say, "My hat."*
   - *He knew that toddlers have a hard time sharing and taking turns.*
   - *The hats were arranged so Lovette could get the hat herself.*

2. How did Mr. Lewis help Lovette and Adam learn about themselves?
   - *He told Lovette where to find another hat so she could have one, too.*
   - *He knelt with them so they could look in the mirror together.*
   - *He pointed out that there were two firefighters and used their names to identify them.*

Providing Experiences That Allow Children to Be Successful

Zora Can Do It!

1. Why did Ms. Gonzalez watch Zora from a slight distance?
   - *She wanted to see what Zora could do on her own, before stepping in.*
   - *She wanted Zora to have a chance to use her own skills.*

2. Why did Ms. Gonzalez decide to give Zora some help?
   - *She saw that Zora was getting frustrated.*
   - *She wanted Zora to experience success, and Zora needed a little help to accomplish the task.*

Building Supportive Relationships With Individual Children

Luci Loves Yogurt

1. How did Ms. Bates use feeding time to build a supportive relationship with Luci?
   - *She responded to Luci's cooing.*
   - *She repeated what Luci's mommy said to her.*
   - *She focused most of her attention on Luci.*

2. What did Ms. Bates do and say to encourage Luci's sense of self?
   - *She offered Luci her own spoon.*
   - *She suggested that they take turns with their spoons.*
   - *She mentioned Luci's mother in connection with an enjoyable eating experience.*

Answer Sheets

Learning Activity A

Using Your Knowledge of Young Infants (Birth–8 Months)

Young Infants ...	What I Do to Support Young Infants' Physical Development
form strong attachments to family members and teachers	*Get to know individual babies: what they like and don't like, how they respond to different stimuli, and how their families meet their needs at home. Care for a small group of infants over as long a period of time as I can.*
smile and coo on their own initiative and in response to others	*Look at infants when diapering and feeding them so they can see my face. Use these one-on-one times to talk with infants and listen to their responses. Read simple books and play games with infants.*
turn their heads and look away when not interested in an activity or toy	*Allow infants to decide what materials to play with and when. When they are not interested, say, "Okay. You don't want to do that. Let's try something else." Then try to interest them in something else.*
discover and learn to control the movement of their hands and other body parts	*Comment on infants' new skills. Hold out toys for them to grasp. Hang up toys for them to kick. Begin to offer finger foods that they can pick up and eat on their own.*
like to be held, cuddled, and amused by simple games and toys	*Hold infants often throughout the day. Talk about different things that I show them in the room and outdoors. Play peek-a-boo and bounce infants on my knee. Sing and recite rhymes. Play together with different toys that invite infants to touch, taste, and otherwise explore.*

Using Your Knowledge of Mobile Infants (8–18 Months)

Mobile Infants ...	What I Do to Support Mobile Infants' Physical Development
respond differently to different people they know and may exhibit stranger anxiety	*Limit the number of people who come into the room (other than family members) so infants won't be overwhelmed or scared. Help infants get to know new people at their own paces. Work with colleagues to make sure that each infant has a primary teacher who understands and has a supportive relationship with the child.*
watch people, objects, and activities in their environment	*Talk with infants about what they see. Help them get involved if they want, by doing an activity with them. Move toys close to them so they can reach them if they want to use them.*
become attached to favorite items such as stuffed animals or blankets	*Respect how infants feel about their favorite things and help them keep these items safe. Allow them to use these items to comfort themselves, as needed. Help children get involved in interesting activities when they are ready to put the item away.*
move from one place to another by creeping, crawling, or walking	*Set up the environment so children can move safely from place to place and so we don't have to tell them no. Applaud their efforts and share their joy in learning new skills. Let infants gain skills at their own pace.*
understand many more words than they can say	*Talk with infants about what they are doing, what other children are doing, and what you are doing. Give simple directions that they can follow to include them in routines, such as, "Lift up your arms." Make and read books about familiar people, objects, and experiences.*

Using Your Knowledge of Toddlers (18–36 Months)

Toddlers ...	What I Do to Support Toddlers' Physical Development
like doing things for themselves most of the time	*Encourage toddlers to take part in routines and to do things for themselves as much as they are able. Provide equipment and materials so they can be independent, such as a sturdy step stool and child-size brooms. Teach toddlers how to do things such as brushing their teeth. Accept that toddlers sometimes want me to do things for them.*
learn to use the toilet on their own	*Recognize the signs that a toddler is ready for toilet learning. Work with the child's family to offer a positive, developmentally appropriate approach at home and at the center. Be patient and encouraging. Accept accidents as a normal part of learning something new.*
begin to notice individual characteristics such as gender and skin color	*Read books and talk with children about their own physical characteristics and those of other people. Discuss how people are the same and how they are different. Answer toddlers' questions, e.g., "Andrew has brown hair like his daddy."*
say *no* when adults ask them to do something	*Play silly games that let children answer* no. *For example, ask, "Do you wear mittens on your ears?" Recognize that saying* no *is a way that toddlers assert their desire to be independent. Offer two choices when possible, e.g., "Would you like an apple or a pear?" "Do you want to play in the sandbox or ride trikes?"*
use words such as *my* and *mine* frequently	*Provide individual cubbies so toddlers can have a place to store their belongings. Provide duplicates of popular items so toddlers don't have to share or take turns before they are ready. Accept that insisting on* my *and* mine *is the toddlers' way of establishing themselves as separate persons.*

Feedback

You will use this *Feedback Summary* many times as you complete the sections of this module. Feedback is an important part of this training program because it helps you check your understanding, apply knowledge, and build skills. You may seek feedback from your colleagues, your trainer, or members of a child's family. When an *Answer Sheet* is provided, you may also compare your ideas to example answers. Remember that there can be more than one good answer to a question.

This chart lists some feedback sources and provides space for notes. Each time you get feedback, describe, in the appropriate column, how it was provided (e.g., discussing your responses to learning activities, feedback after your interactions with children have been observed, written comments). This will help you remember to get feedback from a variety of sources and in a number of ways.

Section	Source of Feedback				
	Colleague	Trainer	Child's Family	Answer Sheet	Other
Overview					
Your Own Social Development					
Pre-Training Assessment					
A. Using Your Knowledge of Infants and Toddlers to Promote Social Development					
B. Creating an Environment That Supports Social Development					
C. Helping Infants and Toddlers Learn to Care About Others					
D. Supporting Children's Play					
Reflecting on Your Learning					

Overview

☐ **Answer** the following questions about the three *Overview* examples in module 9 of *Caring for Infants & Toddlers*.

☐ **Compare** your answers to those on the *Answer Sheet* provided in section 9-10.

☐ **Share and get feedback** on your responses. **Chart** your feedback in section 9-1.

When you are finished, read *Your Own Social Development* in module 9 of *Caring for Infants & Toddlers*.

Creating an Environment That Helps Children Develop Social Skills

Ricky Finds Lovette's Sneaker

1. How did Mr. Lewis use a daily routine (getting ready to go outside) to help children develop social skills?

2. What social skills did the children practice as they prepared to go outside?

Providing Opportunities for Children to Enjoy and Appreciate Other People

Sammy Wants Some Company

    1. How did Ms. Bates figure out what Sammy wanted?

    2. How did Ms. Bates help Sammy learn about enjoying someone's company?

Helping Children Get Along With Each Other

Peter and Malou Read Together

    1. How did Ms. Gonzalez include both Peter and Malou in an activity?

    2. What did Ms. Gonzalez teach the children about relationships with other people?

Your Own Social Development

☐ **Answer** the questions about your own social skills.

☐ **Give** some examples of ways you and your colleagues model social skills and how the children respond to your behavior.

☐ **Share and discuss** your responses. **Chart** your feedback in section 9-1.

When you are finished, complete the section 9-4, *Pre-Training Assessment*.

How do positive relationships at work make your job more enjoyable and rewarding?

Which social skills of other people do you value?

Which of your own social skills do you value?

Which of your social skills would you like to improve? How can you improve them?

Your Own Social Development, continued

In the chart below, give an example of how you and your colleagues model each social skill and explain how the children respond to your behavior. Complete the last row with a social skill of your own choosing.

Social Skill	How We Model It	How the Children Respond
Sharing		
Cooperating		
Helping		

Pre-Training Assessment

☐ **Read** this list of strategies that teachers use to support the social development of infants and toddlers. Refer to the glossary in *Caring for Infants & Toddlers* if you need definitions of the terms that are used.

☐ **Record** whether you do these things *regularly*, *sometimes*, or *not enough*, by checking the appropriate boxes below.

☐ **Review** your answers.

☐ **List** 3–5 skills you would like to improve or topics you would like to learn more about. (When you finish this module, you will list examples of your new or improved knowledge and skills.)

☐ **Share and get feedback** on your responses. **Chart** your feedback in section 9-1.

When you are finished, begin *Learning Activity A, Using Your Knowledge of Infants and Toddlers to Promote Social Development*, in module 9 of *Caring for Infants & Toddlers*.

Creating an Environment That Helps Children Develop Social Skills

check the appropriate box — regularly / sometimes / not enough

	regularly	sometimes	not enough
1. Provide play materials that can be used by more than one child at a time.	☐	☐	☐
2. Encourage children to be helpful.	☐	☐	☐
3. Include simple, homelike props that encourage beginning forms of pretend play.	☐	☐	☐
4. Provide duplicates of popular items so children can play without having to share.	☐	☐	☐
5. Respond to children's communications.	☐	☐	☐

Providing Opportunities for Children to Enjoy and Appreciate Other People

check the appropriate box — regularly · sometimes · not enough

6. Plan daily jobs so one or two children can work together with a teacher. ☐ ☐ ☐

7. Use routines as opportunities to interact with individual children. ☐ ☐ ☐

8. Play with children to model social and pretending skills. ☐ ☐ ☐

9. Involve children in simple activities that involve cooperation. ☐ ☐ ☐

10. Help children value the contributions of others. ☐ ☐ ☐

Helping Children Get Along With Each Other

check the appropriate box — regularly · sometimes · not enough

11. Pay attention to children's expressions of feelings and respond appropriately to show them how to get along with others. ☐ ☐ ☐

12. Introduce spoken language children can use to express what they want and how they feel. ☐ ☐ ☐

13. Model ways to express feelings by sharing your own. ☐ ☐ ☐

14. Explain how another child might be feeling. ☐ ☐ ☐

15. Help children learn how to treat others well. ☐ ☐ ☐

Skills to Improve or Topics to Learn More About

☐ **Read** the following charts that list some typical characteristics of young infants, mobile infants, and toddlers that are important to consider when promoting children's social development.

☐ **Write** examples of what you do to help infants and toddlers develop social skills. You might describe how you arrange your classroom or outdoor area, provide toys and materials, handle routines, interact with children, and partner with families. If you need help getting started, read the completed chart in section 9-10.

☐ **Share and get feedback** on your responses. **Chart** your feedback in section 9-1.

☐ **Add** more examples to the charts as you complete the rest of the learning activities in this module and learn more about promoting children's social development.

When you are finished, begin *Learning Activity B, Creating an Environment That Supports Social Development*, in module 9 of *Caring for Infants & Toddlers*.

Using Your Knowledge of Young Infants (Birth–8 Months)

Young Infants ...	What I Do to Support Young Infants' Social Development
enjoy being held and cuddled	*Hold and cuddle infants during routines such as bottle feedings, while reading, and frequently at other times throughout the day. Let babies know that I enjoy holding and cuddling them. Respond to babies' communicating, through their actions, that they are ready to be put down.*
recognize and smile at the sight of familiar faces and things	
pay attention to the actions and sounds of children and adults	
smile, coo, and babble with familiar people	
ask for attention by crying, laughing, and smiling and through other vocalizations and actions	

Using Your Knowledge of Mobile Infants (8–18 Months)

Mobile Infants ...	What I Do to Support Mobile Infants' Social Development
look to adults for encouragement, support, and approval	*Serve as a base so children can check back with me if they want. Share my pleasure and interest in their relationships with other children. For example, I might say, "It looked like you and Chris were having fun, crawling through the tunnel together."*
like to be near favorite adults and included in daily routines	
follow simple requests and understand more language than they can express	
are increasingly aware of their possessions	
may experience and express a fear of strangers	

From *Skill-Building Journal for Caring for Infants & Toddlers, Module 9, Social.*
©2005 Teaching Strategies, Inc., Washington, DC 20015, www.TeachingStrategies.com

Learning Activity A, continued

Using Your Knowledge of Infants and Toddlers to Promote Social Development

Using Your Knowledge of Toddlers (18–36 Months)

Toddlers...	What I Do to Support Toddlers' Social Development
have strong feelings and may use physical actions—instead of speech—to express anger and frustration	*Observe toddlers carefully and step in if necessary to prevent harm. Get to know individual children and the signs that they are frustrated or angry. Redirect them to a soothing activity when necessary. Help toddlers learn to name their feelings by introducing new vocabulary, for example, "I am angry," or "I am sad." Encourage toddlers to use spoken language to tell others how they feel.*
begin to learn about taking turns and waiting but should not be expected to share without great difficulty	
interact with other children for longer periods and exchange roles in the action when they play together	
engage in simple forms of pretend play	
begin to use caring behaviors to help and comfort others	

From *Skill-Building Journal for Caring for Infants & Toddlers, Module 9, Social*.
©2005 Teaching Strategies, Inc., Washington, DC 20015, www.TeachingStrategies.com

Learning Activity B

9 | Social

Creating an Environment That Supports Social Development

☐ **Read** the list of environmental characteristics that support social development.

☐ **Read** the example about how a teacher changed the environment to support social development.

☐ **Select** one of the listed environmental characteristics as your focus for this activity.

☐ **Describe** your present environment as it relates to the characteristic. **Explain** how it does or does not support social development. **Note** how you would like to change your environment.

☐ **Implement** one of the changes and answer the questions about what happened.

☐ **Share and get feedback** on your responses. **Chart** your feedback in section 9-1.

When you are finished, begin *Learning Activity C, Helping Infants and Toddlers Learn to Care About Others*, in module 9 of ***Caring for Infants & Toddlers***.

Characteristics of Environments That Support Social Development

- Teachers' positive relationships with individual children help them feel valued and loved.
- Teachers play with children to show them that it can be fun to interact someone else.
- Teachers smile, babble, and talk with children during routines and activities.
- Teachers let children know they care about their well-being and want to help them.
- Teachers model caring behavior as they interact with children and adults.
- Teachers help children begin and continue pretend play, as needed.
- The environment has some features that stay the same.
- The environment can be rearranged to meet children's changing needs.
- There are small protected places, indoors and outdoors.
- There are safe places where young infants can watch other people.
- There are places where children and teachers can take a break from the action.
- There are places where two or three children can play side by side or together.
- There are large open areas where mobile infants and toddlers can move and play.
- There are simple, familiar props and dress-up clothes for pretend play.
- There are multiples of children's favorite play materials.
- There are items that can be enjoyed by more than one child at a time.
- There are things that remind children of life at home with their families.

How Our Environment Supports Social Development—Example

Characteristic of the environment: *There are places where two or three children can play side by side or together.*

What does the environment provide now? How does this support social development?

We have a small table and two chairs where two children can sit together to use playdough, do a puzzle, and so on.

Our rocking boat allows two children to rock together.

The sandbox is large enough for several children to play at a time.

What change will you make and why?

We need more variety and something that can be used by one-year-olds as well as toddlers. I will ask the maintenance staff to bring us the large cardboard box from the center's new water heater. I'll open it at both ends so the children can crawl through it. I'll also put some new, brightly colored, washable cushions and stuffed animals inside.

How did the children respond to the change?

Charles (12 months) went to the box right away, looked through one end, and then crawled all of the way through. Ella (15 months) followed right behind. They laughed together and repeated this over and over. This attracted the attention of another child, who joined them.

The next day, some children chose to sit inside the box. That caused a problem for the children who wanted to crawl through. I brought in a smaller box and set it up for the children who wanted a place to sit.

How did the change support children's social development?

Going through the tunnel became a very popular game, and several children could do it together. One child initiated playing follow-the-leader through the tunnel. This meant the children had to cooperate and take turns as they played together. Having two boxes—one for a hideaway and one as a tunnel—meant there were choices and the children did not have to wait for a turn.

How Our Environment Supports Social Development

Characteristic of the environment: _____

What does the environment provide now? How does this support social development?

What change will you make and why?

How did the children respond to the change?

How did the change support children's social development?

☐ **Read** the example below, to help you think about how infants and toddlers begin to show that they care about others.

☐ **Observe** the children in your care for 5-minute periods, several times a day, for three days.

☐ **Review** your notes and list examples of children's learning to use caring behaviors. Explain how you or a colleague modeled or reinforced these behaviors.

☐ **Write** a story about the children's caring about others. Illustrate the story with photographs, pictures, or drawings.

☐ **Read** the story with a few children and **record** their responses.

☐ **Share and get feedback** on your responses. **Chart** your feedback in section 9-1.

When you are finished, complete *Learning Activity D, Supporting Children's Play*, in module 9 of *Caring for Infants & Toddlers*.

Helping Children Learn Caring Behaviors—Example

List examples of children's caring behaviors. Explain how you or your colleague modeled or reinforced caring behaviors.

Aaron (19 months) handed Michael (same age) a shovel in the sandbox. I said, "Aaron, you gave Michael a shovel. You knew he wanted to use one. That was a friendly thing to do."

David (12 months) turned around when he heard me say, "Ouch!" after bumping my knee. He came over to see what had happened. I asked for his help rubbing the sore spot.

Karen (3 months) was crying when she woke up. Lance (12 months) came over to us, looking puzzled. I knelt down while holding Karen. Lance stroked Karen's hair. I said, "You are helping Karen feel better."

Two toddlers were putting toys away at pick-up time. I went over and helped them. Then I said, "We worked well together! Now all of the toys are back on the shelf where the children can find them."

Caring About Others: A Story—Example

Title: *The Day Toby Helped Jan Clean Up Her Spilled Milk*

How did you create the story?

I wrote a story about the time Jan accidentally knocked over a glass of milk. Toby was sitting across from Jan. He got up, brought her some paper towels, and they mopped up the milk together.

To illustrate the story, I decided to divide a large piece of paper into four panels like a comic strip. To illustrate the panels, I recreated the original setting (without the children), took digital photos, and glued the photos to the panels. Then I made puppets by gluing photos of Toby and Jan onto tongue depressors. I moved the puppets against the panel backdrop as I told the story.

What happened when you read the story with the children?

I read the story and used the Toby and Jan puppets to illustrate it. Toby and Jan took a turn with the puppets, and then other children had a turn. I left the panels and puppets out for the rest of the day, so the children could use them on their own. Toby and Jan showed their families at the end of the day.

Helping Children Learn Caring Behaviors

List examples of children's caring behaviors. Explain how you or your colleague modeled or reinforced caring behaviors.

Caring About Others: A Story

Title: _____

How did you create the story?

What happened when you read the story with the children?

9
Social

Learning Activity D
Supporting Children's Play

☐ **Read** the example that follows, to assist your thinking about supporting children's play.

☐ **Select** two children—an infant and a toddler—to be the focus of this activity.

☐ **Observe** each child at play with other children and with another teacher, several times over a 3-day period.

☐ **Review** your notes about each observation.

☐ **Describe** the play, the social skills being used or developed, and what the teacher did to support the child's play.

☐ **Share and get feedback** on your responses. **Chart** your feedback in section 9-1.

When you are finished, complete section 9-10, *Reflecting on Your Learning.*

Supporting Children's Play—Example

Child(ren): _Toby_   **Age(s):** _15 months_   **Date/Time:** _June 12; 2:00 p.m._

Setting: _Outdoors in play yard_   **Teacher:** _Mr. Lewis_

Describe the play.

Toby and Mr. Lewis are throwing a ball into a laundry basket. They take turns and laugh when the ball goes in the basket. Toby tries to get the ball out, but he can't reach it. Mr. Lewis watches to see what Toby will do. Toby tries to climb into the basket, but he won't fit. Then he tips over the basket, and the ball rolls out. He picks up the ball and runs back to Mr. Lewis. Mr. Lewis hugs Toby and tells him, "You solved the problem by yourself."

What social skills was the child developing or using?

Toby learned that it is fun to play with someone else. He learned about taking turns during a game. He learned that he can solve problems on his own and that Mr. Lewis will be there if he needs him. He learned that Mr. Lewis enjoys his company.

What did the teacher do to support the child(ren)'s play?

Mr. Lewis took turns with Toby. He laughed with him and let him know he likes playing with him. He let him solve the problem on his own. He showed Toby that he knows Toby is capable.

Supporting Children's Play

Child(ren): _____ **Age(s):** _____ **Date/Time:** _____

Setting: _____ **Teacher:** _____

Describe the play.

What social skills was the child developing or using?

What did the teacher do to support the child(ren)'s play?

Reflecting on Your Learning

You have now completed all of the learning activities for this module. Whether you are a new or experienced teacher, you have gained new understandings and developed new skills for helping infants and toddlers build social skills. As you complete the steps below, chart your feedback in section 9-1.

☐ **Review** the log you kept in *Learning Activity A, Using Your Knowledge of Infants and Toddlers to Promote Social Development*. **Add** to the log more examples of infants and toddlers gaining social skills.

☐ **Review** your responses to the *Pre-Training Assessment* for this module and **complete** section 9-9b, "Summarizing Progress."

☐ **Explore some curriculum connections.** You will use the skills you developed through module 9, *Social*, when implementing a curriculum. Look through your program's curriculum to see how it addresses this topic. For example, *The Creative Curriculum® for Infants & Toddlers* has some sections you might want to review:

- Chapter 1, *Building Relationships: The Focus of Your Work*
- Chapter 7, *Creating a Welcoming Environment*

☐ **Build partnerships with families.** Share what you learned in this module with the families of the children in your care. Here are some suggestions:

- Plan and lead a family workshop on engaging children in play and supporting social skills such as sharing and taking turns. Use information from the Web sites of organizations that support children's play.
  - The Alliance for Childhood (www.allianceforchildhood.org) offers online resources about play.
  - Playing for Keeps (www.playingforkeeps.org) offers a free *Family Guide to Play* brochure and poster.
- Make a list of toys and other play materials that encourage children to play with family members and other children. Share the list with families.
- Create a handout for families about the many ways children can play with a cardboard box. Illustrate it with photos of the children in your group playing with a box.

☐ **Complete the assessments.** Tell the trainer who is guiding you through the modules that you are ready for the knowledge and competency assessments.

☐ **Start a new module.** After completing the assessments successfully, it is time to move on. Congratulations on your progress so far, and good luck with the next module.

Reflecting on Your Learning

Summarizing Progress

Name:_____ **Date:**_____

Did completing this module make you more aware of how you help infants and toddlers build social skills? List the strategies you use.

How did you share something you learned with families?

What did you learn about an individual child?

What curriculum connections did you explore?

What do you want to learn more about, and how will you do it?

Creating an Environment That Helps Children Develop Social Skills

Ricky Finds Lovette's Sneaker
1. How did Mr. Lewis use a daily routine (getting ready to go outside) to help children develop social skills?
   - *He invited two children to help another child find her lost shoe.*
   - *He asked who would help carry the big bag of balls.*
   - *He pointed out that carrying a big bag is easier when they help each other.*

2. What social skills did the children practice as they prepared to go outside?
   - *They learned to help another child.*
   - *They learned to work together to complete a task: carrying the bag.*
   - *They learned to wait until everyone is ready to go outside, because all of the children are important.*

Providing Opportunities for Children to Enjoy and Appreciate Other People

Sammy Wants Some Company
1. How did Ms. Bates figure out what Sammy wanted?
   - *She bent down to talk with him and lifted him from the crib.*
   - *She checked his diaper and his chart on the bulletin board.*

2. How did Ms. Bates help Sammy learn about enjoying someone's company?
   - *She held and tried to comfort him.*
   - *She took him to look at the bird outside the window.*
   - *She sat with him, helping him stand on her lap.*

Helping Children Get Along With Each Other

Peter and Malou Read Together
1. How did Ms. Gonzalez include both Peter and Malou in an activity?
   - *She paid attention to Malou and asked if she wanted to sit and read, too.*
   - *She made room on her lap so they could all look at the book together.*

2. What did Ms. Gonzalez teach the children about relationships with other people?
   - *She taught them that three people can enjoy the same activity (reading) at the same time.*
   - *She helped Peter understand that Malou also has needs and interests.*
   - *She helped them understand that it is enjoyable to talk about pictures together.*

Using Your Knowledge of Young Infants (Birth–8 Months)

Young Infants ...	What I Do to Support Young Infants' Social Development
enjoy being held and cuddled	*Hold and cuddle infants during routines such as bottle feedings, while reading, and frequently at other times throughout the day. Let babies know that I enjoy holding and cuddling them. Respond to babies' communicating, through their actions, that they are ready to be put down.*
recognize and smile at the sight of familiar faces and things	*Look at children when talking with them. Smile back when they smile at me. Engage them in play and conversation; pause while talking so they can coo and gurgle in turn. Notice the toys and other items they are looking at. Bring the items closer so they can see them better and, if appropriate, handle them.*
pay attention to the actions and sounds of children and adults	*Place infants where they can watch other children. Talk with the infants about what they see and hear, for example, "Jeff and Macy are rolling cars on the rug," and "Mr. Lewis is changing Yancey's diaper." Let infants touch each other while I sit nearby to make sure everyone is safe.*
smile, coo, and babble with familiar people	*Respond to infants' communications. Introduce songs and rhymes and talk with infants to help them expand their communication skills. Use routines as opportunities to explain what I am doing and to have conversations about all kinds of topics.*
ask for attention by crying, laughing, and smiling and through other vocalizations and actions	*Pay attention to children's cries, figure out what they need, and respond accordingly. Watch for other cues that they want attention from me or another teacher. Stay current with the new ways they are learning to express themselves.*

Using Your Knowledge of Mobile Infants (8–18 Months)

Mobile Infants ...	What I Do to Support Mobile Infants' Social Development
look to adults for encouragement, support, and approval	*Serve as a base so children can check back with me if they want. Share my pleasure and interest in their relationships with other children. For example, I might say, "It looked like you and Chris were having fun, crawling through the tunnel together."*
like to be near favorite adults and included in daily routines	*Respond to infants who follow me to different places. Involve infants in daily chores such as putting out a new box of tissues. Talk about what I am doing and show infants how to help. Examine all of our routines and identify ways to include the mobile infants.*
follow simple requests and understand more language than they can express	*Talk with infants, even if they don't respond with speech. Give simple 1- or 2-step directions such as, "Please give Nora this rattle." Ask infants to help during routines. For example, say, "Please hold up your arm. Great! Here comes the sleeve."*
are increasingly aware of their possessions	*Provide individual, accessible storage places for children's personal belongings where they know their possessions will be safe and easy to reach.*
may experience and express a fear of strangers	*Ask people whom children do not know to approach slowly. Explain to strangers that some of the children might be afraid of them. Stay with a frightened child when he or she is getting to know a new person. Understand the child's feelings, label them with words, and talk about them. "You don't know Mr. Trent, so he seems scary. I will help you get to know him."*

Answer Sheets

Learning Activity A, continued

Using Your Knowledge of Toddlers (18–36 Months)

Toddlers...	What I Do to Support Toddlers' Social Development
have strong feelings and may use physical actions—instead of speech—to express anger and frustration	*Observe toddlers carefully and step in if necessary to prevent harm. Get to know individual children and the signs that they are frustrated or angry. Redirect them to a soothing activity when necessary. Help toddlers learn to name their feelings by introducing new vocabulary, for example, "I am angry," and "I am sad." Encourage toddlers to use spoken language to tell others how they feel.*
begin to learn about taking turns and waiting but should not be expected to share without great difficulty	*Offer multiples of favorite play items to minimize the need for toddlers to share and take turns. Involve toddlers in enjoyable activities where they use toys and materials with other children.*
interact with other children for longer periods and exchange roles in the action when they play together	*Set up the environment with areas just large enough for 2–3 children to use at a time, such as a small table with two chairs. Offer toys and materials that are more fun when used by more than one person, such as balls and wagons. Encourage toddlers to help each other, for example, to carry something heavy, find a lost shoe, or pass the toothpaste.*
engage in simple forms of pretend play	*Provide simple, familiar props and dress-up clothes. Watch children at play and help as needed to get things started, involve a bystander, or keep the play going. Offer new items to extend the play or to suggest different ways of pretending. Invite children to pretend during other activities. For example, ask them to meow and move like cats while I join in.*
begin to use caring behaviors to help and comfort others	*Model caring behaviors such as sharing, taking turns, and helping, and talk about what I am doing. Comment on toddlers' use of caring behaviors, for example, by saying, "I saw you take turns hugging the big bear. Taking turns was a good idea."*

10
Guidance

Feedback

You will use this *Feedback Summary* many times as you complete the sections of this module. Feedback is an important part of this training program because it helps you check your understanding, apply knowledge, and build skills. You may seek feedback from your colleagues, your trainer, or members of a child's family. When an *Answer Sheet* is provided, you may also compare your ideas to example answers. Remember that there can be more than one good answer to a question.

This chart lists some feedback sources and provides space for notes. Each time you get feedback, describe, in the appropriate column, how it was provided (e.g., discussing your responses to learning activities, feedback after your interactions with children have been observed, written comments). This will help you remember to get feedback from a variety of sources and in a number of ways.

Section	Source of Feedback				
	Colleague	Trainer	Child's Family	Answer Sheet	Other
Overview					
Your Own Self-Discipline					
Pre-Training Assessment					
A. Using Your Knowledge of Infants and Toddlers to Guide Their Behavior					
B. Understanding and Responding to Children's Temperaments					
C. Using a Positive Guidance Approach					
D. Preventing and Responding to Problem Behavior					
Reflecting on Your Learning					

Overview

☐ **Answer** the following questions about the three *Overview* stories in module 10 of *Caring for Infants & Toddlers*.

☐ **Compare** your answers to those on the *Answer Sheet* provided in section 10-10.

☐ **Share and get feedback** on your responses. **Chart** your feedback in section 10-1.

When you are finished, read *Your Own Self-Discipline* in module 10 of *Caring for Infants & Toddlers*.

Providing an Environment That Supports the Development of Self-Control

Jon Falls Asleep At Last

1. How did Ms. Bates and Ms. Gonzalez support each other?

2. What did Ms. Bates and Ms. Gonzalez do to help Jon?

Helping Children Understand and Manage Their Feelings

Zora Uses Words

1. How did Zora feel when Lovette took her orange slice?

2. How did Mr. Lewis help Zora learn to express her feelings in an acceptable way?

Using Positive Guidance to Help Children Gain Self-Control

Adam Throws Safely

1. What did Ms. Bates know about Adam?

2. How did Ms. Bates guide Adam's behavior?

Your Own Self-Discipline

☐ **List** a few examples of how self-discipline guides your behavior at work.

☐ **List** a few examples of how self-discipline guides your behavior at home.

☐ **Answer** the questions that follow.

☐ **Share and get feedback** on your responses. **Chart** your feedback in section 10-1.

When you are finished, complete the section 10-4, *Pre-Training Assessment*.

List a few examples of how self-discipline guides your behavior at work.

List a few examples of how self-discipline guides your behavior at home.

Think of a time when you did not use self-control. What affected your loss of control?

What does your own experience tell you about what children need if they are to gain self-control?

Pre-Training Assessment

☐ **Read** this list of strategies that teachers use to guide the behavior of infants and toddlers. Refer to the glossary in *Caring for Infants & Toddlers* if you need definitions of the terms that are used.

☐ **Record** whether you do these things *regularly*, *sometimes*, or *not enough*, by checking the appropriate boxes below.

☐ **Review** your answers.

☐ **List** 3–5 skills you would like to improve or topics you would like to learn more about. (When you finish this module, you will list examples of your new or improved knowledge and skills.)

☐ **Share and get feedback** on your responses. **Chart** your feedback in section 10-1.

When you are finished, begin *Learning Activity A, Using Your Knowledge of Infants and Toddlers to Guide Their Behavior,* in module 10 of *Caring for Infants & Toddlers.*

Providing an Environment That Supports the Development of Self-Control

check the appropriate box — regularly — sometimes — not enough

1. Provide safe, well-organized spaces that let children make choices and use materials. ☐ ☐ ☐

2. Follow a flexible schedule so teachers can respond promptly to children's needs. ☐ ☐ ☐

3. Plan daily routines and activities to minimize waiting time. ☐ ☐ ☐

4. Create visible, cozy areas where a child, or a child and a teacher, can spend time alone. ☐ ☐ ☐

5. Prepare children for changes and transitions. ☐ ☐ ☐

Helping Children Understand and Manage Their Feelings

check the appropriate box — regularly / sometimes / not enough

6. Teach children words to name their feelings. ☐ ☐ ☐

7. Model appropriate ways to identify and express feelings. ☐ ☐ ☐

8. Read books, tell stories, and talk about feelings. ☐ ☐ ☐

9. Accept and respond to the feelings expressed through crying, words, other vocal sounds, and gestures. ☐ ☐ ☐

10. Offer materials and activities that may calm and soothe children who are upset. ☐ ☐ ☐

Using Positive Guidance to Help Children Gain Self-Control

check the appropriate box — regularly / sometimes / not enough

11. Get to know and understand each child's temperament. ☐ ☐ ☐

12. Use simple, positive statements that tell children what to do, rather than only what not to do. ☐ ☐ ☐

13. Redirect children from unwanted to acceptable behavior. ☐ ☐ ☐

14. Anticipate problem behaviors and take steps to prevent them. ☐ ☐ ☐

15. Look for the reasons behind a child's problem behavior. ☐ ☐ ☐

Skills to Improve or Topics to Learn More About

☐ **Read** the following chart that lists some typical characteristics of young infants, mobile infants, and toddlers that are related to guiding their behavior.

☐ **Write** examples of what you do to guide the behavior of infants and toddlers. You might describe how you arrange your classroom or outdoor area, provide toys and materials, handle routines, interact with children, and partner with families. If you need help getting started, read the completed chart in section 10-10.

☐ **Share and get feedback** on your responses. **Chart** your feedback in section 10-1.

☐ **Add more examples** to the chart as you complete the rest of the learning activities in this module and learn more about guiding children's behavior.

When you are finished, begin *Learning Activity B, Understanding and Responding to Children's Temperaments*, in module 10 of *Caring for Infants & Toddlers*.

Using Your Knowledge of Young Infants (Birth–8 Months)

Young Infants ...	What I Do to Support Young Infants' Physical Development
cry to express physical discomfort, boredom, or stress	*Respond to infants immediately so I can find out what they need and provide it. Watch and listen to infants to learn what their different cries mean. Work with colleagues so infants do not have to wait for someone to come to their aid.*
respond to faces and voices	
reach out and grab things that might not be safe	
learn to wait for a short time and to comfort themselves if their needs have been met consistently	
use their growing skills to make things happen	

Using Your Knowledge of Mobile Infants (8–18 Months)

Mobile Infants ...	What I Do to Support Mobile Infants' Physical Development
experience and express a wide range of feelings	*Talk with infants in a calm, respectful tone of voice. Label and talk about their feelings and the feelings of other children, e.g., "Did you hear Joey laugh? He's happy to have a clean diaper."*
are interested in other children	
know how their families and teachers feel about them	
watch and learn from the important adults in their lives	
learn to move their bodies in new ways	

Using Your Knowledge of Toddlers (18–36 Months)

Toddlers …	What I Do to Support Toddlers' Physical Development
admire and want to please adults	*Acknowledge their positive behavior by describing it, e.g., "I saw you hang your coat on the hook," and "You passed the crayon basket to your friend." Invite toddlers to help me with tasks such as wiping the table before lunch or moving chairs out of the way so we can dance.*
want to make decisions for themselves	
test limits and often say *no*	
experience a range of emotions	
are sometimes overwhelmed by intense feelings and may behave in ways that hurt other children or adults	

☐ **Read** the example below to guide your thinking about various aspects of temperament.

☐ **Answer** the questions about your own temperament. Describe yourself by choosing a number on a scale of 1–5 for each question. Both ends of the scale are defined for each question.

☐ **Choose** a child with whom you have had difficulty building a supportive relationship to be the focus of this activity. Use the form provided to **keep** a log of your interactions with this child during routines and play for the next three days. You may copy the form.

☐ **Review** the entries in your log. Then **answer** the questions that follow about the child's temperament and how your relationship is affected by both your temperament and the child's.

☐ **Share and get feedback** on your responses. **Chart** your feedback in section 10-1.

When you are finished, begin *Learning Activity C, Using a Positive Guidance Approach*, in module 10 of *Caring for Infants & Toddlers*.

Thinking About Your Own Temperament

Intensity (responding to the world)

You are on a trip and staying in a hotel. How do you respond to sleeping in this new setting?

I have no problems   *I wear ear plugs and bring my own pillow*

1 ☐   2 ☐   3 ☐   4 ☐   5 ☐

Activity level (getting to know and take part in the world)

Think about what you like to do on breaks, in your spare time, or on vacation. What kind of activities do you like?

I like to sit, watch, and listen   *I like to move and do as much as possible*

1 ☐   2 ☐   3 ☐   4 ☐   5 ☐

Persistence (handling frustration)

Imagine yourself tackling a home repair job. Things are not going well. The parts won't fit together, you can't figure out how to use the tools, and your family is counting on your fix-it skills. What happens next?

I call a professional repair person   *I keep trying until I figure it out*

1 ☐   2 ☐   3 ☐   4 ☐   5 ☐

Coping with change (responding to new people, routines, and environments)

You just learned that a new teacher will be working with you. Imagine yourself getting to know this person. What do you do? How do you feel?

I wait to be approached   *I offer a big welcome to our center*

1 ☐   2 ☐   3 ☐   4 ☐   5 ☐

Think about your responses to the questions above. How does your temperament affect your relationships with the infants and toddlers in your care?

Log of Interactions With a Child

Child: _____ **Age:** _____ **Dates:** _____

What the Child Did	What I Did and Said
Routine/Activity: Time:	
Routine/Activity: Time:	
Routine/Activity: Time:	

Understanding Temperament

What did you learn about this child's temperament?

How is your temperament similar to the child's? How is it different?

How might the child's temperament affect your relationship with him or her?

How can you use what you learned about your temperament and the child's unique characteristics to offer positive guidance?

How can you get to know and appreciate the unique characteristics of all of the children in your group?

☐ **Read** the example below to assist your thinking about a positive guidance approach.

☐ **Choose** a mobile infant or toddler to be the focus of this activity.

☐ **Observe** the child over a 3-day period. **Take** notes on the child's behavior, the possible reason for the behavior, and your positive guidance.

☐ **Read** your notes and describe what your learned from the experience. Explain how you can apply this learning to offer positive guidance.

☐ **Share and get feedback** on your responses. **Chart** your feedback in section 10-1.

When you are finished, complete *Learning Activity D, Preventing and Responding to Problem Behavior*, in module 10 of *Caring for Infants & Toddlers*.

Using a Positive Guidance Approach—Example

Child: *Tina*　　　　　**Age:** *24 months*　　　**Observer:** *Ms. Bates*

Date/Time: *May 22; 11:15 a.m.*　　　**Setting:** *Outdoors*

Child's Behavior	Possible Reasons for the Behavior	Positive Guidance
Tina grabbed a watering can from Henry, who was using it to water our garden.	*Tina wants to water the plants that we planted yesterday. She doesn't know how to ask for a turn. We only have one watering can.*	*I bent down and said, "Tina, I know you want to water the plants. Henry is using the watering can now." Then I offered an alternative, "Here's a pitcher from the water table. You may use it to water the plants."*

How can you use what you learned about this child to promote his or her self-control?

Tina and a few other children were running and climbing while we planted the garden. I didn't think they were interested. I should have remembered that anything having to do with water is a popular activity for this age group. I will stop at the dollar store on my way home and pick up some more watering cans.

I also learned that Tina will accept an alternative item. She is more interested in watering the plants than in the container she uses to hold the water.

Using a Positive Guidance Approach

Child: _____ Age: _____ Observer: _____

Day One

Date/Time: _____ Setting: _____

Child's Behavior	Possible Reasons for the Behavior	Positive Guidance

Day Two

Date/Time: _____ Setting: _____

Child's Behavior	Possible Reasons for the Behavior	Positive Guidance

Day Three

Date/Time: _____ Setting: _____

Child's Behavior	Possible Reasons for the Behavior	Positive Guidance

How can you use what you learned about this child to promote his or her self-control?

☐ **Read** the example below of how a teacher responded to an ongoing problem behavior.

☐ **Choose** a child in your care who has an ongoing behavioral problem to be the focus of this activity.

☐ **Describe** the behavior and how you and your colleagues respond.

☐ **Discuss** the situation with the child's family.

☐ **Develop** a plan for responding to the behavior at home and at the center.

☐ **Share and get feedback** on your responses. **Chart** your feedback in section 10-1.

When you are finished, complete section 10-9, *Reflecting on Your Learning.*

Responding to an Ongoing Problem Behavior—Example

Child: *Frances*   **Age:** *30 months*   **Date:** *June 25*

What behavior is an ongoing problem?

Frances bites other children, usually on their arms.

How long and how often has the child been behaving this way?

This has been going on for about two weeks. It happens about every other day.

In what situations does it happen? Provide an example.

Frances bites when she is in small, confined spaces. For example, she was crawling through the box tunnel, and another child crawled in from the other side. When he got close to her, she bit him.

How do you respond now?

One teacher comforts the child who was bitten and gets some ice. So far we have not needed more first aid than that. The other teacher takes Frances aside and tells her that she may not bite people, that it hurts the other person, and that she should use words to express her feelings. We ask if she wants to help get the ice for the injured child. Then we try to get her engaged in an activity in an open space that will allow her to release some of her feelings. Throwing bean bags in a box has been a helpful strategy.

How does the child respond?

She cries and seems sad, rather than angry. Sometimes she sucks her thumb. Usually she wants to help get the ice.

Answer the following questions after your discussion with the child's family.

Did something happen at the center that might have upset the child?

We can't think of anything that changed.

Did something happen at home that might have upset the child?

The family recently moved to a new townhouse. Frances continues to share a room with her younger sister. Frances's family says that she likes the new neighborhood. Their house is right across the street from a park where Frances loves to play with her mom and sister.

What might be causing the problem behavior?

Frances might feel most comfortable in open settings where she doesn't feel confined. It might be related to getting used to the new house and neighborhood, even though she seems to like them. Maybe she is picking up on the tension we are beginning to feel about her biting.

What are your plans for responding to this behavior at home and at the center?

I met with Frances's family. She doesn't bite at home, but her family will reinforce what we say and do at the program. They will help her practice using speech to express her feelings. Frances talks well, so she can tell others what she wants and needs.

At the center, we will continue to watch Frances and take steps to prevent her from feeling confined in small places. She loves crawling through the tunnel so, when she does, one of us will step in as necessary. We will remind the children about the limits we set for safety, including crawling through the tunnel in only one direction. We will make sure that the interest areas have two entries/exits so children do not feel trapped. We will respond as before if Frances does bite or hurt anyone.

What happened at home and at the center when you tried your plans? Has the behavior changed or stopped?

Frances's mom has noticed that Frances stops playing and comes over to her when older children come into the park. She thinks Frances doesn't like it when things get crowded, busy, and noisy. After we intervened a few times to keep Frances from being in small spaces with other children and after we reminded her to use speech, her biting stopped. Taking a good look at the cause and agreeing on a unified approach at home and at the center made a big difference. Addressing this issue has decreased the tension that Frances may have been picking up on. Our attention has helped Frances remember to say, "Too close," when another child gets too close to her.

Responding to an Ongoing Problem Behavior

Child: _____ **Age:** _____ **Date:** _____

What behavior is an ongoing problem?

How long and how often has the child been behaving this way?

In what situations does it happen? Provide an example.

How do you respond now?

How does the child respond?

Answer the following questions after your discussion with the child's family.

Did something happen at the center that might have upset the child?

Did something happen at home that might have upset the child?

What might be causing the problem behavior?

What are your plans for responding to this behavior at home and at the center?

What happened at home and at the center when you tried your plans? Has the behavior changed or stopped?

Reflecting on Your Learning

You have now completed all of the learning activities for this module. Whether you are a new or experienced teacher, you have gained new understandings and developed new skills for guiding the behavior of infants and toddlers. As you complete the steps below, chart your feedback in section 10-1.

☐ **Review the chart** you began in *Learning Activity A, Using Your Knowledge of Infants and Toddlers to Guide Their Behavior*. Think about the new ideas you learned as you completed the learning activities in this module. **Add to the chart** examples of things you did while working on this module to guide infants' and toddlers' behavior.

☐ **Review your responses** to the *Pre-Training Assessment* for this module and **complete** section 10-9b, "Summarizing Progress."

☐ **Explore some curriculum connections.** You will use the skills you developed through module 10, *Guidance*, when implementing a curriculum. Look through your program's curriculum to see how it addresses this topic. For example, *The Creative Curriculum® for Infants & Toddlers* has some sections you might want to review:

• Chapter 1, *Building Relationships: The Focus of Your Work*

• Chapter 10, *Guiding Children's Behavior*

☐ **Build partnerships with families.** Share what you learned in this module with the families of the children in your care. Here are some suggestions:

• Let every family know that you appreciate their child as an important member of the group. Share stories about the important and minor things the child does, particularly those that highlight the child's uniqueness. Encourage families to share information with you, too, so their children will be supported by strong, responsive partnerships.

• Provide information about infant and toddler development in a number of ways. For example, weave it into daily conversations; write an e-mail newsletter; share books, articles, and videos; direct families to helpful Web sites; and create bulletin boards that depict children using different skills in a variety of routines and activities.

• While maintaining confidentiality, acknowledge and respond to families' concerns about guiding their children's behavior. Discuss experiences at home and at the center. Offer practical information to help them accept, appreciate, and build on their children's unique characteristics. Help families recognize their own strengths in supporting their children's development and learning.

☐ **Complete the assessments.** Tell the trainer who is guiding you through the modules that you are ready for the knowledge and competency assessments.

☐ **Start a new module.** After completing the assessments successfully, it is time to move on. Congratulations on your progress so far, and good luck with the next module.

Reflecting on Your Learning

Summarizing Progress

Name:_____ **Date:**_____

Did completing this module make you more aware of what you do to guide the behavior of infants and toddlers? List the strategies you use.

How did you share something you learned with families?

What did you learn about an individual child?

What curriculum connections did you explore?

What do you want to learn more about, and how will you do it?

Providing an Environment That Supports the Development of Self-Control

Jon Falls Asleep At Last

1. How did Ms. Bates and Ms. Gonzalez support each other?
   - *They took turns caring for Jon.*
   - *They worked together to find out how to comfort Jon and help him fall asleep.*

2. What did Ms. Bates and Ms. Gonzalez do to help Jon?
   - *Ms. Bates fed Jon, changed his diaper, and put him on his back to sleep.*
   - *Ms. Gonzalez held him on her shoulder and patted his back.*
   - *Both teachers let Jon know that they would help him feel better.*

Helping Children Understand and Manage Their Feelings

Zora Uses Words

1. How did Zora feel when Lovette took her orange slice?
   - *angry*
   - *frustrated*
   - *out of control*

2. How did Mr. Lewis help Zora learn to express her feelings in an acceptable way?
   - *He put his arm out to stop Zora from hitting Lovette.*
   - *He stated what Zora wanted.*
   - *He encouraged Zora to use speech to tell Lovette not to take the orange.*

Using Positive Guidance to Help Children Gain Self-Control

Adam Throws Safely

1. What did Ms. Bates know about Adam?
   - *Adam likes to throw things, and he throws fairly well.*
   - *Adam can make choices when presented with two options.*
   - *Adam likes to be active.*

2. How did Ms. Bates teach Adam positive behavior?
   - *She walked over and bent down to talk to him.*
   - *She acknowledged that he was learning to throw well.*
   - *She explained what would happen if he hit someone.*
   - *She let him choose between two options: to throw safely on the grass or to do something else.*

Answer Sheet
Learning Activity A

Using Your Knowledge of Young Infants (Birth–8 Months)

Young Infants ...	What I Do to Support Young Infants' Physical Development
cry to express physical discomfort, boredom, or stress	*Respond to infants immediately so I can find out what they need and provide it. Watch and listen to infants to learn what their different cries mean. Work with colleagues so infants do not have to wait for someone to come to their aid.*
respond to faces and voices	*Smile at infants and respond to their smiles. Talk to them while feeding, diapering, and playing with them. Wait for them to respond and then continue our conversation. Let them know through speech and nonverbal language that I like their company. Hold and carry them so they can see the other children.*
reach out and grab things that might not be safe	*Offer safe toys where they can find them. Remove small objects and place unsafe items out of their reach. Check the room and outdoors regularly to make sure the environment is safe for their explorations.*
learn to wait for a short time and to comfort themselves if their needs have been met consistently	*Meet their needs promptly and regularly so they can learn to rely on me. Talk with them to let them know that I am on my way to help them. "I hear you crying. I am bringing your bottle. I know you are hungry." Talk with families often to find out what works at home to comfort and support each baby.*
use their growing skills to make things happen	*Provide toys that let infants explore cause and effect, such as rattles they can shake to make noise or a ball to roll across the grass. Talk with infants about what they did and what happened next, e.g., "You pushed the ball, so it rolled all the way over there. Let's go get it."*

From *Skill-Building Journal for Caring for Infants & Toddlers, Module 10, Guidance.*
©2005 Teaching Strategies, Inc., Washington, DC 20015, www.TeachingStrategies.com

Using Your Knowledge of Mobile Infants (8–18 Months)

Mobile Infants ...	What I Do to Support Mobile Infants' Physical Development
experience and express a wide range of feelings	*Talk with infants in a calm, respectful tone of voice. Label and talk about their feelings and the feelings of other children, e.g., "Did you hear Joey laugh? He's happy to have a clean diaper."*
are interested in other children	*Guide infants to show them how to touch each other gently. Say, "Be gentle." Model how to enjoy being with other people. Play with two children at the same time to help them get to know and have fun with each other.*
know how their families and teachers feel about them	*Throughout the day, tell infants how I feel about them, verbally and by the way I meet their needs. I also show and tell them that what they do is important to me and to their families. "Look at you, standing up! Your legs are getting so strong."*
watch and learn from the important adults in their lives	*Let infants see and learn from my positive interactions with colleagues, other children, and their families. Express and talk about my own feelings in appropriate ways. Talk about simple problems and what I do to solve them without getting frustrated. "That was the last tissue. I'll have to get a new box from the cabinet. Whoops, I'm too short. I need the step stool."*
learn to move their bodies in new ways	*Stay alert to and remove potential hazards, inside and outdoors. Make sure that mobile infants have safe places to practice moving (out of the way of young infants and walking toddlers). Offer an outstretched hand to new walkers, but understand when infants do not want or need assistance.*

Using Your Knowledge of Toddlers (18–36 Months)

Toddlers...	What I Do to Support Toddlers' Physical Development
admire and want to please adults	*Acknowledge their positive behavior by describing it, e.g., "I saw you hang your coat on the hook," and "You passed the crayon basket to your friend." Invite toddlers to help me with tasks such as wiping the table before lunch or moving chairs out of the way so we can dance.*
want to make decisions for themselves	*Offer toddlers simple, meaningful choices as often as I can so they can feel a sense of control over their lives. Encourage them to choose which book to read, which toys to play with, which tricycle to ride, and so on.*
test limits and often say no	*Avoid power struggles. Let toddlers make decisions for themselves as often as possible. Remain flexible except when necessary to ensure safety. Set clear limits and apply them consistently. Invite toddlers to help me do things. Ask silly questions so they can have fun saying* no *without causing problems.*
experience a range of emotions	*Name toddlers' feelings for them and encourage them to use speech to express themselves. Talk about my own feelings and those of other children. Read stories about emotions, and talk about how the characters felt and what they did. Help toddlers gradually learn acceptable ways of managing emotions.*
are sometimes overwhelmed by intense feelings and may behave in ways that hurt other children or adults	*Step in right away to stop aggressive behavior. For example, calmly but firmly say, "Hitting hurts. I won't let you hit anyone, and I won't let anyone hit you. Use words to tell us what you want and how you feel." I make sure my facial expressions and other body language tell the toddler that I am serious. Later I talk about what happened and help the child practice using speech. If our strategies do not to help the child, I involve the family in figuring out what is going on and how to address it.*

Feedback

You will use this *Feedback Summary* many times as you complete the sections of this module. Feedback is an important part of this training program because it helps you check your understanding, apply knowledge, and build skills. You may seek feedback from your colleagues, your trainer, or members of a child's family. When an *Answer Sheet* is provided, you may also compare your ideas to example answers. Remember that there can be more than one good answer to a question.

This chart lists some feedback sources and provides space for notes. Each time you get feedback, describe, in the appropriate column, how it was provided (e.g., discussing your responses to learning activities, feedback after your interactions with children have been observed, written comments). This will help you remember to get feedback from a variety of sources and in a number of ways.

Section	Source of Feedback				
	Colleague	**Trainer**	**Child's Family**	**Answer Sheet**	**Other**
Overview					
Your Own Views About Families					
Pre-Training Assessment					
A. Building Partnerships With Families					
B. Resolving Differences					
C. Offering Ways for Families to Be Involved					
D. Planning and Holding Conferences With Families					
E. Providing Support to Families					
Reflecting on Your Learning					

☐ **Answer** the following questions about the *Overview* stories in module 11 of *Caring for Infants & Toddlers.*

☐ **Compare** your answers to those on the *Answer Sheet* provided in section 11-11.

☐ **Share and get feedback** on your responses. **Chart** your feedback in section 11-1.

When you are finished, turn to *Your Own Views About Families* in module 11 of *Caring for Infants & Toddlers.*

Developing a Caregiving Partnership With Each Family

Luci Pulls Herself Up

1. What are some signs that Ms. Gonzalez and Luci's father have a strong partnership?

2. How does Luci benefit from their strong partnership?

Offering A Variety of Ways for Families to Be Involved in the Program

Sammy's Mother Updates the Newsletter

1. How did Ms. Bates help Sammy's mother handle her feelings about leaving Sammy?

2. How did Ms. Bates help Sammy's mother find a way to participate in his life at the program?

Providing Support to Families

Mr. Lewis Reaches Out to Zora's Mother

1. What did Mr. Lewis do and say to offer support to Ms. Trent?

2. Why will Mr. Lewis ask his colleagues for their ideas before calling Ms. Trent?

Your Own Views About Families

☐ **Think** about your past and present experiences as a member of a family.

☐ **Answer** the following questions and **consider** how your views about families and the pressures they experience affect your work with families.

☐ **Share and discuss** your responses. **Chart** your feedback in section 11-1.

When you are finished, complete section 11-4, *Pre-Training Assessment.*

Whom did you consider to be part of the family in which you grew up?

How are the families of the children in your care similar to and different from your own family?

What pressures affect parents today? How do they affect your work with families?

How do your own views about families affect your work?

Pre-Training Assessment

☐ **Read** this list of strategies that teachers use to build partnerships with families. Refer to the glossary in *Caring for Infants & Toddlers* if you need definitions of the terms that are used.

☐ **Record** whether you do these things *regularly*, *sometimes*, or *not enough*, by checking the appropriate boxes below.

☐ **Review** your answers.

☐ **List** 3–5 skills you would like to improve or topics you would like to learn more about. (When you finish this module, you will list examples of your new or improved knowledge and skills.)

☐ **Share and get feedback** on your responses. **Chart** your feedback in section 11-1.

When you are finished, begin *Learning Activity A, Building Partnerships With Families*, in module 11 of *Caring for Infants & Toddlers*.

Developing a Caregiving Partnership With Each Family

check the appropriate box   *regularly*   *sometimes*   *not enough*

1. Exchange positive and current information about each child's routines and activities every day. ☐ ☐ ☐

2. Invite and respond to families' questions and concerns. ☐ ☐ ☐

3. Get to know a little about each family. ☐ ☐ ☐

4. Use information provided by families to meet individual needs. ☐ ☐ ☐

5. Plan jointly with families to offer children consistency and security at home and at the program. ☐ ☐ ☐

Offering a Variety of Ways for Families to Be Involved in the Program

check the appropriate box · regularly · sometimes · not enough

6. Encourage families to visit the program at any time. ☐ ☐ ☐

7. Invite families to share their talents, interests, home languages, and aspects of their cultures. ☐ ☐ ☐

8. Offer a variety of family-involvement opportunities to accommodate individual schedules, interests, and skills. ☐ ☐ ☐

9. Hold meetings and events at times that are convenient for most families. ☐ ☐ ☐

10. Offer workshops and resources on topics of interest to families. ☐ ☐ ☐

Providing Support to Families

check the appropriate box · regularly · sometimes · not enough

11. Maintain confidentiality about children and families. ☐ ☐ ☐

12. Recognize when families are under stress and offer additional support. ☐ ☐ ☐

13. Encourage families to relax and enjoy their children. ☐ ☐ ☐

14. Help families recognize what their children learn through daily routines and activities. ☐ ☐ ☐

15. Share information about child development and typical behaviors of infants and toddlers. ☐ ☐ ☐

16. Use familiar terms, instead of professional jargon, when communicating with families. ☐ ☐ ☐

17. Notify a supervisor when a family seems to need professional help. ☐ ☐ ☐

Skills to Improve or Topics to Learn More About

SECTION **11-5a**

Learning Activity A
Building Partnerships With Families

☐   **Read** the following example of how a teacher became acquainted with a family and used her knowledge to build a partnership.

☐   **Select** a family that you want to know better and decide on the best ways of doing so. **Think** about what you already know about the family and their child. **Prepare** a list of questions you will ask, **explain** what else you will do to get to know them better, and **try** your ideas.

☐   **Record** what you learned about this family and their child, and **explain** how you used this information to build a partnership.

☐   **Share and get feedback** on your responses. **Chart** your feedback in section 11-1.

When you are finished, begin *Learning Activity B, Resolving Differences*, in module 11 of *Caring for Infants & Toddlers.*

Building Partnerships With Families—Example

A family I want to get to know better: _____*The Wilsons*_____

What I know now about this family:

The Wilsons have one child, Sharon, 16 months. Mrs. Wilson is five months pregnant. Both Mr. and Mrs. Wilson work during the day. I rarely see them. Mrs. Wilson's mother lives in their neighborhood. She often drops Sharon off or picks her up, but she seems very uncomfortable and shy. I would like to talk with Sharon's parents and her grandmother about what Sharon does each day and to learn more about what she is like at home.

I will use these approaches to get to know this family better:

I will take photos of Sharon to send home. On the back of the photos, I will write about what she was doing and learning. I will also include a note saying that I will soon call them during the evening, to see if we can set up a time to talk.

I will ask these questions to get to know the family better:

- *What do you want Sharon to do and learn in child care?*
- *What kinds of things does she most enjoy doing at home? What upsets her?*
- *How should we communicate about what Sharon is doing at home and in child care?*

What I learned about the family and their child:

The Wilsons work long hours and are trying to save some extra money before their new, unexpected baby arrives. They are sorry they don't have time to spend in our program. They were afraid Sharon's grandmother would not be welcome and had asked her to stay out of our way.

We decided that we would talk on the phone in the evening once a month. Mrs. Wilson talked with her mother, Mrs. Carson, and Mrs. Carson would like to volunteer for one morning a week. She has wanted to spend more time at the program but was afraid to say anything to me.

They want Sharon to explore and play. Because they don't have much time, they don't allow her to do messy activities, but they told me they are happy to send in extra clothes and hope that she will have the chance to play with dough, water, sand, and maybe even some paint.

They also have e-mail and said they would be very glad to receive some photos of Sharon playing.

How I plan to use what I learned to build a partnership with the family:

I am going to welcome Mrs. Carson and let her know how much she will be helping us by going on walks, setting up lunch, etc. At first she will probably want plenty of time with Sharon. Once Sharon gets used to her presence, I hope Mrs. Carson will want to do more with other children as well.

I will keep taking photos of Sharon exploring and playing—especially doing messy activities— to e-mail to her parents. I will also send photos of Mrs. Carson.

I will be sure to let them know about the coming family meeting where we will provide dinner and child care.

After implementing your plans, answer the following questions.
How have you been able to build a partnership with the family? How has this helped you work together to support the child?

Mrs. Carson loves being with us each week. She says it makes her feel special and important. Knowing that Sharon's grandmother is so welcomed makes the Wilsons feel more comfortable talking with me. They also feel as though they are contributing to the program.

We talk by phone regularly now, and Mr. Wilson came to our parent meeting. They are happy to see that Sharon is having fun in our program—and getting messy. They are worried about how to help Sharon get ready for the new baby. They said they had not been setting limits for her lately because they were feeling guilty. We have been talking about how setting limits helps toddlers feel safe and loved, and the Wilsons say that makes sense to them. They also said that having someone to talk with makes parenting much easier.

Building Partnerships With Families

A family I want to get to know better: _____

What I know now about this family:

I will use these approaches to get to know this family better:

I will ask these questions to get to know the family better:

What I learned about the family and their child:

How I plan to use what I learned to build a partnership with the family:

After implementing your plans, answer the following questions.
How have you been able to build a partnership with the family? How has this helped you work together to support the child?

☐ **Write** about a time when you had a difference of opinion with a family or about how you handled a misunderstanding.

☐ **Share and get feedback** on your responses. **Chart** your feedback in section 11-1.

When you are finished, begin *Learning Activity C, Offering Ways for Families to Be Involved*, in module 11 of *Caring for Infants & Toddlers*.

Resolving a Difference of Opinion or a Misunderstanding—Example

Describe a time when you had a difference of opinion or a misunderstanding with a family.

The Yuans asked me not to give Lisa (21 months) a nap during the day because they were having a hard time getting her to go to sleep at night. I explained that she gets very tired and fussy by the end of the day when she doesn't sleep during the day, and that I think a nap is important for her.

What caused the difference or misunderstanding?

The Yuans are both going to school and working. They need to study at night and feel pressured to get Lisa to sleep.

I stated my opinion because I think it is best for Lisa to get some rest during the day. Also, Lisa gets very cranky when she doesn't sleep, and the whole afternoon is harder for everyone.

How did you handle the situation?

We agreed that I would put Lisa in her crib each day. If she fell asleep, that would be fine. If she didn't, I would lift her out to play. After a week, we would talk again about whether this strategy is a good idea. Lisa fell asleep on two days. On the other three, her parents said she kicked and cried on their way home and bedtime was still a struggle. They agreed that I should help her settle into sleep by rubbing her back. We talked about how worrying about getting Lisa to bed at night might make it harder. We also talked about developing a routine to make bedtime easier. Mr. Yuan suggested playing some Chinese music so they can relax and then read a story together.

How did you emphasize the child's interests in the decision-making process?

I figured that Lisa must be very tired when she falls asleep and that our arrangement would let her get some sleep. We were all taking good care of Lisa by giving our plan only one week before checking with each other to see how it was working for Lisa and her family.

Were you satisfied with the ways things turned out? If not, how will you handle a future difference of opinion or misunderstanding?

Yes, I think things worked out for everyone.

Resolving a Difference of Opinion or a Misunderstanding

Describe a time when you had a difference of opinion or a misunderstanding with a family.

What caused the difference or misunderstanding?

How did you handle the situation?

How did you emphasize the child's interests in the decision-making process?

Were you satisfied with the ways things turned out? If not, how will you handle a future difference of opinion or misunderstanding?

☐ **Choose** a family involvement strategy: your own idea, one suggested by families, or one from *Caring for Infants & Toddlers*, module 11, *Learning Activity C*. **Discuss** your selection with supervisors and other teachers and ask for their ideas about implementing the strategy.

☐ **Develop a plan** for implementing the strategy and tracking family responses. **Use** the form provided to record your strategy, plans, results, and follow-up.

☐ **Share and get feedback** on your responses. **Chart** your feedback in section 11-1.

When you are finished, begin *Learning Activity D, Planning and Holding Conferences With Families*, in module 11 of *Caring for Infants & Toddlers*.

Family Involvement Strategy—Example

Strategy:

We have a tape player, but most tapes are too expensive for the program to buy or they are intended for older children. Family members will record favorite songs that are appropriate for very young children. To go with the tapes, we will make family photo albums for each child.

Plans:

I will send a notice home, asking family members—including grandparents and siblings—to participate. The program will supply blank tapes. The songs can be family favorites. I'll try to make sure we tape a variety of songs in the different languages and from the different cultures of our families.

I will also ask each family to bring in photos of people, places, and pets that are important to their child. We will make a book for each child about her family. If families do not have photos to share, we will take them with our camera.

Results:

Four families volunteered to make tapes. Each family taped several songs, so now we have a nice selection. The children really enjoy hearing their families' voices on tape. One family made their tape at a family reunion. Each family said they would be happy to make more tapes whenever we need them.

Follow-up:

I will make this an ongoing family-involvement project. I am going to be sure to share observations of how much children enjoy the tapes. I plan to play the tape at our next family workday, to show families that they do not have to be professional singers and to see if anyone else would like to participate. I will keep the tape recorder and tapes out, in case families want to make tapes at the program. I would love to have a tape from each family so every child can hear the voices of people he loves while he is at the program.

Family Involvement Strategy

Strategy:

Plans:

Results:

Follow-up:

☐ **Schedule a conference** with a family to share information about their child and to discuss development and learning.

☐ **Prepare** for the conference by organizing the child's portfolio, summarizing what you know about the child's development, and thinking about what aspects of development you want to focus on next.

☐ **Conduct** the conference. **Add** families' observations about their child to the "Summary of Developmental Progress" form, and **determine** next steps together. **Share** and **record** ideas about how to support the child at home and at the program.

☐ **Evaluate** the conferences and **explain** what, if anything, you will do differently next time.

☐ **Share and get feedback** on your responses. **Chart** your feedback in section 11-1.

When you are finished, begin *Learning Activity E, Providing Support to Families*, in module 11 of *Caring for Infants & Toddlers*.

Preparing for and Conducting the Conference

Child/Age: _____ **Family member(s) attending:** _____

Date of conference: _____ **Date of last conference:** _____

What activities does this child enjoy most?

What makes this child happy?

What upsets this child?

Concerns (if any):

Summary of Developmental Progress

Child: _____   Date: _____

Area of Development	Observations	Next Steps
Social/Emotional (developing a positive sense of self; relating positively to others)		
Physical (gaining control of large and small muscles)		
Cognitive (learning how things work, classifying, problem solving, and pretend play)		
Language (listening, speaking, and exploring reading and writing)		

Conference Evaluation

How did you establish a relaxed tone?

What information did you share so that the family understands what a typical day at the program is like for their child?

How did you show respect for the family's style of communication?

What was the same and different about how you and the family view the child's development and learning?

Were you asked for advice? If so, how did you respond?

What did you and the family decide to focus on next as you support the child's development and learning?

How did you end the conference?

In what ways did this conference help you to build a partnership with the family to support the child's learning and development?

What information did the family share with you that will help you evaluate your program?

What, if anything, will you do differently next time?

☐ **Read** the following example about supporting a family.

☐ **Focus** on times when you offer support to families during the next two weeks.

☐ **Reflect** on what parents requested, what you thought they needed, how you responded, and the outcome. **Make** as many copies of the blank form as needed to **record** your supportive experiences with families.

☐ **Share and get feedback** on your responses. **Chart** your feedback in section 11-1.

When you are finished, complete section 11-10, *Reflecting on Your Learning.*

Reaching Out to Families—Example

Child: _Larry_   **Age:** _21 months_   **Date:** _October 23_

Problem:

Larry is very jealous of his new baby sister, Elizabeth. His parents said that he hits and pinches her. One day they stopped him just as he was about to dump her out of her bouncy seat. They are very angry with him. They have no idea that this kind of behavior is not unusual.

Help that the family requested or that I thought was needed:

Help the adults have more realistic expectations about Larry's feelings and behavior. Support Larry. Keep Elizabeth safe.

My response:

I assured Larry's parents that Larry's behavior is typical of a young child who has a new sibling. I suggested that Larry needs special time with family members, away from the new baby.

I asked whether there are any patterns in his behavior before Larry tries to hurt his sister. Does he try to hurt her when he is tired or hungry or when the two children are left alone?

I suggested that they talk with the Greenes, who also have a toddler and a new baby and who have offered to talk with other parents about their experiences. I loaned them some simple books to read to Larry about having a new baby in the family. I also said we would talk about new babies during the day when, for example, we see a baby during a walk or Larry plays with a doll.

The outcome:

The family says it was helpful to talk with a family in the same situation. They have begun to spend extra time with Larry alone. Larry is not as upset, and he really likes story time with his dad.

Reaching Out to Families

Child: _____ **Age:** _____ **Date:** _____

Problem:

Help that the family requested or that I thought was needed:

My response:

The outcome:

Reflecting on Your Learning

You have now completed all of the learning activities for this module. Whether you are a new or experienced teacher, you have gained new understandings and developed new skills for building partnerships and communicating with families. Before going on to the next module, take a few minutes to think about what you have learned. As you complete the steps below, chart your feedback in section 11-1.

☐ **Review your responses** to the *Pre-Training Assessment* for this module and complete section 11-10b, "Summarizing Progress."

☐ **Explore some curriculum connections.** You will use the skills you developed through module 11, *Families*, when implementing a curriculum. Look through your program's curriculum to see how it addresses this topic. For example, *The Creative Curriculum® for Infants & Toddlers* has some sections you might want to review:

- Chapter 1, *Building Relationships: The Focus of Your Work*, "Building Relationships with Families"

- Chapter 5, *Planning and Evaluating Your Program*, "Goals and Objectives for Working with Families"

- Chapter 6, *Individualizing for Children and Families*, "Goals for Working with Families Form"

- Many chapters include example letters to families, to suggest a way to share information about how your program relates to various aspects of child development.

☐ **Complete the assessments.** Tell the trainer who is guiding you through the modules that you are ready for the knowledge and competency assessments.

☐ **Start a new module.** After completing the assessments successfully, it is time to move on. Congratulations on your progress so far, and good luck with the next module.

Summarizing Progress

Name:_____ **Date:**_____

Did completing this module make you more aware of what you do to build partnerships and communicate with families in your program? List the strategies you use.

Do you view your work with families any differently now? Explain your response.

In what ways did completing this module help you build partnerships with families?

What curriculum connections did you explore?

What do you want to learn more about, and how will you do it?

Developing a Caregiving Partnership With Each Family

Luci Pulls Herself Up

1. What are some signs that Ms. Gonzalez and Luci's father have a strong partnership?
   - *Luci's father seems comfortable, sitting in the overstuffed chair in the room.*
   - *He shares Luci's accomplishment with Ms. Gonzalez, and she responds.*

2. How does Luci benefit from their strong partnership?
   - *She will stay safe because both her family and her teachers know about her new ability to move from place to place.*
   - *Luci will know that many people care about her and respond to her accomplishments.*

Offering a Variety of Ways for Families to Be Involved in the Program

Sammy's Mother Updates the Newsletter

1. How did Ms. Bates help Sammy's mother deal with her feelings about leaving Sammy?
   - *She listened while Sammy's mother talked about missing him while she is at work.*
   - *She showed Sammy's mother a photograph of Sammy.*

2. How did Ms. Bates help Sammy's mother find a way to participate in his life at the program?
   - *Ms. Bates asked for her help in sharing photographs of the children with other families.*
   - *Ms. Bates accepted her suggestion to scan the photos for the newsletter so everyone can see what their children do at the program.*

Providing Support to Families

Mr. Lewis Reaches Out to Zora's Mother

1. What did Mr. Lewis do and say to offer support to Ms. Trent?
   - *He sat next to her on the bench so he could listen to her concern.*
   - *He said that Zora has been fussing at the program.*
   - *He suggested that they plan a time to talk.*
   - *He agreed to talk by phone during the evening.*

2. Why do you think Mr. Lewis will ask his colleagues for their ideas before calling Ms. Trent?
   - *His colleagues' observation notes may provide useful information about when Zora gets fussy.*
   - *They may have suggestions that he has not thought of, so he will have more ideas to share with Ms. Trent.*

Feedback

You will use this *Feedback Summary* many times as you complete the sections of this module. Feedback is an important part of this training program because it helps you check your understanding, apply knowledge, and build skills. You may seek feedback from your colleagues, your trainer, or members of a child's family. When an *Answer Sheet* is provided, you may also compare your ideas to example answers. Remember that there can be more than one good answer to a question.

This chart lists some feedback sources and provides space for notes. Each time you get feedback, describe, in the appropriate column, how it was provided (e.g., discussing your responses to learning activities, feedback after your interactions with children have been observed, written comments). This will help you remember to get feedback from a variety of sources and in a number of ways.

Section	Source of Feedback				
	Colleague	**Trainer**	**Child's Family**	**Answer Sheet**	**Other**
Overview					
Managing Your Own Life					
Pre-Training Assessment					
A. Getting to Know Each Child					
B. Organizing and Using Portfolios					
C. Responding to Each Child's Needs and Interests					
D. Working as a Team to Plan and Evaluate the Program					
Reflecting on Your Learning					

Overview

Program Management

☐ **Answer** the following questions about the *Overview* stories in *Caring for Infants & Toddlers*.

☐ **Compare** your answers to those on the *Answer Sheet* provided in section 12-10.

☐ **Share and get feedback** on your responses. **Chart** your feedback in section 12-1.

When you are finished, read *Managing Your Own Life* in module 12 of *Caring for Infants & Toddlers*.

Learning About Each Child

Mr. Lewis Learns by Watching

1. How did Mr. Lewis gather objective and accurate information about Jessica during a daily routine?

2. What did Mr. Lewis learn about Jessica?

Working as a Team to Offer a Program That Meets Each Child's Needs

Three Colleagues Plan as a Team

1. How did Ms. Bates use a team approach to planning?

2. How did the teachers use information from their observations to support individual children and the group?

Evaluating the Program

Three Colleagues Evaluate Their Program

1. What information did Ms. Gonzalez, Ms. Bates, and Mr. Lewis use to evaluate their program?

2. On the basis of their evaluation, what did Ms. Gonzalez, Ms. Bates, and Mr. Lewis decide to do?

Managing Your Own Life

☐ **Think** about how you manage your own life effectively.

☐ **Answer** the following questions.

☐ **Describe** a strategy that you will try in order to manage a frustrating situation.

☐ **Share and get feedback** on your responses. **Chart** your feedback in section 12-1.

When you are finished, complete section 12-4, *Pre-Training Assessment*.

Think about how you manage your own life effectively. What are some of your regular home management strategies, such as refilling the watering cans after your weekly plant watering?

Now think about how you manage your job effectively. What are some of your regular management strategies, such as keeping children's portfolios in plastic containers with lids?

Think about a frustrating situation at home or work, such as spending time each morning searching for your keys or running out of construction paper before the new order is due. Describe the situation and a strategy you could use to solve the problem.

Pre-Training Assessment

☐ **Read** this list of strategies that teachers use to manage programs effectively. Refer to the glossary in *Caring for Infants & Toddlers* if you need definitions of the terms that are used.

☐ **Record** whether you do these things *regularly*, *sometimes*, or *not enough*, by checking the appropriate boxes.

☐ **Review** your responses.

☐ **List** 3–5 skills you would like to improve or topics you would like to learn more about. (When you finish this module, you will list examples of your new or improved knowledge and skills.)

☐ **Share and get feedback** on your responses. **Chart** your feedback in section 12-1.

When you are finished, begin *Learning Activity A, Getting to Know Each Child*, in module 12 of *Caring for Infants & Toddlers*.

Learning About Each Child

check the appropriate box — regularly · sometimes · not enough

1. Communicate with families often, using a variety of strategies. ☐ ☐ ☐

2. Observe children regularly and note your observations. ☐ ☐ ☐

3. Observe children in different settings and at different times of the day. ☐ ☐ ☐

4. Collect examples and photographs that document children's skills, interests, and progress. ☐ ☐ ☐

5. Take advantage of everyday routines and interactions to learn about children's interests and abilities. ☐ ☐ ☐

Pre-Training Assessment, continued

Working as a Team to Offer a Program That Meets Each Child's Needs

check the appropriate box · regularly · sometimes · not enough

6. Meet regularly with colleagues to plan the program. ☐ ☐ ☐

7. Ensure that curriculum goals are the basis for planning experiences for the children. ☐ ☐ ☐

8. Use ongoing assessment information to plan for individual children and the group. ☐ ☐ ☐

9. Include each family in planning ways to support their child's development and learning. ☐ ☐ ☐

10. Use creative thinking skills, such a brainstorming, to plan and to solve problems. ☐ ☐ ☐

11. Appreciate and use the strengths of all team members, including teachers, families, and volunteers. ☐ ☐ ☐

Evaluating the Program

check the appropriate box · regularly · sometimes · not enough

12. Use program goals as a component of program evaluation. ☐ ☐ ☐

13. Identify what is working well and what needs to be improved, every day. ☐ ☐ ☐

14. Use assessment information to plan teaching approaches and to change the environment, interactions, routines, and activities in response to children's individual characteristics. ☐ ☐ ☐

15. Use information about children's use of materials to determine whether changes are needed. ☐ ☐ ☐

Skills to Improve or Topics to Learn More About

Learning Activity A
Getting to Know Each Child

☐ **Read** the following examples of observation notes.

☐ **Select** a child to observe once a day, every day during a one-week period. You might choose a child whom you do not already know very well.

☐ **Observe** the child for 5–10 minutes per day. **Record** your notes on the blank "Observation Form." **Complete** the checklist at the bottom of the form. (You will need a separate form for each observation.)

☐ **Ask** your director, a colleague, or your trainer to observe the child with you at least twice during the week. You will both note information about the same child, at the same time. **Compare** your observation notes after each joint observation.

☐ **Analyze** your observation notes with your co-observer to determine whether they are objective, accurate, and complete. If they are not objective, accurate, and complete, repeat the learning activity and conduct another co-observation.

☐ **Share and get feedback** on your responses. **Chart** your feedback in section 12-1.

When you are finished, begin *Learning Activity B, Organizing and Using Portfolios*, in module 12 of *Caring for Infants & Toddlers*.

Observation Notes—Examples

Child: _Nicholas (N)_   **Age:** _4 months_   **Date/Time:** _May 2; 10:15 a.m._

Observer: _Mr. David_

Setting: _On the patio, with Ms. Jones (Ms. J) other children_

Behavior:

N on belly on blanket. Ms. J walks onto patio singing, "I'll be coming to the patio, Nicholas, Nicholas...." She approaches him from behind, but N does not respond. She walks in front of N and crouches down. N sees her, squeals, and waves his arms and legs.

Child: _Nicholas (N)_   **Age:** _4 months_   **Date/Time:** _May 13; 11:00 a.m._

Observer: _Mr. David_

Setting: _Crib, awaking from morning nap_

Behavior:

N rolls onto side. Looks through crib railing. Rolls on back. Lifts hand toward mobile. Puts hand in mouth. Sucks on fist.

Child: _Nicholas (N)_   **Age:** _4 months_   **Date/Time:** _May 14; 8 a.m._

Observer: _Mr. David_

Setting: _Near the entrance, in cubby area at arrival_

Behavior:

N enters, in grandfather's arms. Grandfather unzips and takes off N's jacket. N smiles at grandfather. Ms. J. holds arms out. Grandfather gives her N. Then Grandfather leaves. N turns head toward door. Ms. J carries N to mat. Places N on tummy, on mat. N looks at self in propped mirror.

Observation Note

Child: _____ **Age:** _____ **Date/Time:** _____

Observer: _____

Setting:

Behavior:

Checklist for the Observation and Note:

☐   I observed during a classroom activity and noted information as it happened or right after.

☐   I recorded all necessary information about the observation: child's name, child's age, date, time, observer's name, setting, and behavior.

☐   The setting information includes the area in which the activity took place and who was involved.

☐   The note includes only information about what I saw and heard. It does not include labels, judgments, or assumptions.

☐   The note includes short phrases, abbreviations, children's initials, arrows to indicate movement, or other shortcuts that make it easier for me to write quickly.

☐   The note includes a brief description of what a child does and says, as well as how the child does and says it.

If you conducted this observation at the same time as a colleague, how does your observation note compare with your co-observer's note?

☐ **Collect** portfolio items over a two-week period, to document the development and learning of the child you observed in *Learning Activity A*. **Develop** a system for storing and organizing the portfolio items.

☐ **Read** the example chart that lists portfolio items and explains why each was included.

☐ **List** the portfolio items that you collected and explain why you included them. Use the blank chart that follows the example.

☐ **Describe** your organizational and storage system in the space provided after your chart.

☐ **Share and get feedback** your responses. **Chart** your feedback in section 12-1.

When you are finished, begin *Learning Activity C, Responding to Each Child's Needs and Interests*, in module 12 of *Caring for Infants & Toddlers*.

Creating a Portfolio—Example

Child: _Audrey_ **Age:** _5 months_ **Dates:** _April 2–16_

Portfolio Item	How It Documents This Child's Development
Photo of Audrey on her blanket in a protected area, watching a toddler who is talking to her.	*Audrey is very interested in other children. Her eyes open wide, and she gets very animated when she sees another child.*
Notes on conversation with Audrey's mother about trip to doctor.	*We were worried about whether Audrey has a full range of wrist movement and discussed this with her family. The doctor said she is fine.*
Photograph of Audrey sitting up and reaching for a nearby toy. Her father is lying on the floor beside her.	*Audrey started sitting by herself week. Now she is able to play when sitting, and to reach for objects with her whole hand. Her family spends as much time with Audrey at the program as they can.*

Describe your system for organizing and storing the portfolio items.

I used an accordion file as the portfolio container. I organized the items by area of development: social/emotional, physical, cognitive, and language.

Creating a Portfolio

Child: _____   Age: _____   Dates: _____

Portfolio Item	How It Documents This Child's Development

Describe your system for organizing and storing the portfolio items.

Learning Activity C
Responding to Each Child's Needs and Interests

☐ **Read** the example answers on the completed "Information Summary" form that follows, to assist your thinking about individual children.

☐ **Select** the child you observed in *Learning Activity A* as the focus for this activity.

☐ **Review** your observation notes from *Learning Activity A*, information from the portfolio you created in *Learning Activity B*, and information that the child's family has provided. Then **analyze** what you know.

☐ **Summarize** what you learned about the child and **answer** the questions on the blank "Information Summary" form that follows the example.

☐ **Read** the completed planning form that is provided, to assist your thinking about meeting the child's individual needs and building on the child's interests.

☐ **Plan** ways to respond to the child's skills, interests, and needs. **Record** your plan on the blank form provided.

☐ **Share and get feedback** on your responses. **Chart** your feedback in section 12-1.

When you are finished, begin *Learning Activity D, Working as a Team to Plan and Evaluate the Program*, in module 12 of *Caring for Infants & Toddlers*.

Information Summary—Example

Child: _Li_   **Age:** _32 months_   **Date:** _March 15_

What do you know about the child's culture, home language, and family?

Li's family is Chinese. She was born in the US. Her grandparents live in China, but some aunts and uncles live near Li. Li hears both Chinese and English at home. Her grandmother will be coming this summer to visit. Her family just got a new puppy.

What are this child's favorite materials, activities, and special interests?

Li loves to help in our program and at home. She also loves to play with sand and water. She is very interested in dogs. She points to pictures of puppies in books and brought in a picture of her puppy, "Lucky," that we taped on the refrigerator.

What information has the child's family provided about his or her development?

Li hears mostly Chinese at home. She speaks a little in both Chinese and English. Her cousins, who are about the same age, live nearby, and the children play together on the weekends when their families get together.

What do you know about the child's social/emotional development?

Li is independent and self-confident. She is beginning to play with other children in our program instead of watching or playing side by side. Li selects and carries out activities of her own choosing. She sometimes names the feelings that she experiences.

What do you know about the child's cognitive development?

Li can do simple puzzles, participate in reading stories aloud, and plan ways to solve simple problems.

What do you know about the child's physical development?

Li is more inclined to choose activities that involve small motor skills, rather than large motor skills. She can string beads and holds crayons in an adult-like grasp. She is also learning to brush her teeth and use a spoon. Li runs, climbs, and jumps when she is offered gentle encouragement and when she knows I am nearby to help her.

What do you know about the child's language development?

Li speaks in two- and three-word phrases and sentences in both English and Chinese. She understands and responds to simple directions, questions, stories and songs in both languages.

Information Summary

Child: _____ **Age:** _____ **Date:** _____

What do you know about the child's culture, home language, and family?

What are this child's favorite materials, activities, and special interests?

What information has the child's family provided about his or her development?

What do you know about the child's social/emotional development?

What do you know about the child's cognitive development?

What do you know about the child's physical development?

What do you know about the child's language development?

Planning for an Individual Child—Example

Child's name: _Li_   **Date:** _Mar. 15_

Program Element	How I Can Meet the Child's Needs
Daily Schedule (the sequence and timing of daily events) **Examples:** Offer opportunities throughout the day for children to choose what to do, what to use, and with whom to play. Whenever possible, care for children individually or in small groups, e.g., to run an errand or take a walk.	_Invite Li to join small-group walks to the park, where an adult can support her while she climbs and jumps._
Materials (toys, books, equipment, and other items available for the children's use) **Examples:** Include materials that correspond to children's cultures, languages, and families. Rotate materials. Add new materials to the environment in response to the children's changing needs, interests, and skill levels.	_Provide more books about dogs and some stuffed dogs for Li's dramatic play._
Environment (indoor and outdoor areas and arrangement of furniture, materials, and equipment) **Examples:** Create a welcoming, environment in which children feel relaxed. Display materials on low shelves so children can make choices. Provide open spaces for active play and protected spaces from which children can watch safely.	_Set up an obstacle course outside. Invite Li to play._

Program Element	How I Can Meet the Child's Needs
Routines (daily events such as cleanup, meals, and naps) **Examples:** Serve milk or juice in small pitchers so children can pour their own drinks or ask for help. Use techniques recommended by parents to help children fall asleep, such as singing or sitting near a child.	*No changes needed.*
Hellos and Goodbyes (arrivals and departures) **Examples:** Greet families and children when they arrive. Encourage families to develop separation and reunion rituals. Be available to help children relate to you and engage in play. Play peek-a-boo and read aloud stories about coming and going.	*No changes needed.*
Learning opportunities (activities you plan and offer; times when children choose to join in an activity planned and led by an adult) **Examples:** Offer activities that allow children to make choices. Plan activities, such as cooking and singing, that correspond with children's cultures, languages, and families.	*Invite Li to use gross motor skills, both indoors and outdoors. Ask Li's family for some simple recipes for a cooking activity. Encourage Li to join in.*
Interactions (verbal and nonverbal communications between teachers and children) **Examples:** Recognize when to help children complete a task and when to allow them to explore on their own. Tailor individual support to the way the child typically handles frustration and challenges.	*Ask Li's family to teach me a few more Chinese words. Model English and Chinese words for objects, animals, and activities whenever possible.*

Planning for an Individual Child

Child's name: _____ Date: _____

Program Element	How I Can Meet the Child's Needs
Daily Schedule (the sequence and timing of daily events) **Examples:** Offer opportunities throughout the day for children to choose what to do, what to use, and with whom to play. Whenever possible, care for children individually or in small groups, e.g., to run an errand or take a walk.	
Materials (toys, books, equipment, and other items available for the children's use) **Examples:** Include materials that correspond to children's cultures, languages, and families. Rotate materials. Add new materials to the environment in response to the children's changing needs, interests, and skill levels.	
Environment (indoor and outdoor areas and arrangement of furniture, materials, and equipment) **Examples:** Create a welcoming, environment in which children feel relaxed. Display materials on low shelves so children can make choices. Provide open spaces for active play and protected spaces from which children can watch safely.	

Program Element	How I Can Meet the Child's Needs
Routines (daily events such as cleanup, meals, and naps) **Examples:** Serve milk or juice in small pitchers so children can pour their own drinks or ask for help. Use techniques recommended by parents to help children fall asleep, such as singing or sitting near a child.	
Hellos and Goodbyes (arrivals and departures) **Examples:** Greet families and children when they arrive. Encourage families to develop separation and reunion rituals. Be available to help children relate to you and engage in play. Play peek-a-boo and read aloud stories about coming and going.	
Learning opportunities (activities you plan and offer; times when children choose to join in an activity planned and led by an adult) **Examples:** Offer activities that allow children to make choices. Plan activities, such as cooking and singing, that correspond with children's cultures, languages, and families.	
Interactions (verbal and nonverbal communications between teachers and children) **Examples:** Recognize when to help children complete a task and when to allow them to explore on their own. Tailor individual support to the way the child typically handles frustration and challenges.	

☐ **Read** the weekly plan example that follows.

☐ **Review** the children's portfolios with your team, including your observation notes and summaries.

☐ **Prepare** a weekly plan on the basis of what you know about the children. Write your plan on the blank form that follows the example.

☐ **Implement** the plan for one week. **Hold** brief meetings several times during the week to evaluate how the plan is working and to make changes if they are needed.

☐ **Answer** the questions on the plan evaluation form.

☐ **Share and get feedback** on your responses. **Chart** your feedback in section 12-1.

When you are finished, complete section 12-9, *Reflecting on Your Learning*.

Weekly Plan—Example

Date: *Week of March 24–28*

Changes to the environment:

Near the tables where we eat, hang pictures of people who are cooking.
Add a few more pots and spoons to the pretend play props.
Organize equipment and materials so we can find what we need.

Special activities I plan to offer this week:

Tuesday: *Invite children to help scrub and later mash potatoes.*
Wednesday: *Invite children to peel and cut bananas.*
Friday: *Make English muffin pizzas. (Have graham crackers and juice ready in case we need to change our plans.)*

Changes to daily routines:

At lunchtime, talk about who made the children's lunches.

Family involvement:

Ask parents to tell us about their experiences while cooking with children at home.

To do:

Ms. Gleason will look through our cookbooks for some simple recipes.
Ms. Williams will bring in her toaster oven on Friday.

Weekly Plan

Date:_____

Changes to the environment:

Special activities I plan to offer this week:

Changes to daily routines:

Family involvement:

To do:

Evaluating Your Weekly Plan

How did infants and toddlers respond to the changes in the environment?

How did children respond to the special activities you offered?

How did children respond to the changes in daily routines?

How were families involved?

Considering what you learned this week, what will you do differently next week?

How can you build on the experiences that children had this week?

Reflecting on Your Learning

You have now completed all of the learning activities for this module. Whether you are a new or experienced teacher, you have gained new understandings and developed new skills for managing your program effectively. Before going on to the next module, take a few minutes to think about what you have learned. As you complete the steps below, chart your feedback in section 12-1.

☐ **Review your responses** to the *Pre-Training Assessment* for this module and complete section 12-9b, "Summarizing Progress."

☐ **Explore some curriculum connections.** You will use the skills you developed through module 12, *Program Management*, when implementing a curriculum. Look through your program's curriculum to see how it addresses this topic. For example, *The Creative Curriculum® for Infants & Toddlers* has some sections you might want to review.

- Chapter 5, *Planning and Evaluating Your Program*, includes ideas about making evaluation a regular part of the planning process.

- Chapter 6, *Individualizing for Children and Families*, includes a discussion about individualizing goals and objectives for children, and it presents a chart of strategies for overcoming obstacles to observation.

☐ **Build partnerships with families.** Share what you learned in this module with the families of the children in your care. Here are some suggestions:

- Discuss with families how and why you observe their children.

- Share your observation notes with families so they can understand their children's experiences at the program.

- Give families a tour of the classroom and outdoor areas and explain how you have set up the environment to meet the needs of their children.

- Display your weekly plans on a bulletin board, discuss them with families, and ask for suggestions.

☐ **Complete the assessments.** Tell the trainer who is guiding you through the modules that you are ready for the knowledge and competency assessments.

☐ **Start a new module.** After completing the assessments successfully, it is time to move on. Congratulations on your progress so far, and good luck with the next module.

Reflecting on Your Learning

Summarizing Progress

Name:_____ **Date:**_____

Did completing this module make you more aware of what you do to manage your program effectively? List your strategies below.

What did you learn that was new and surprising?

What did you learn that you would like to share with families and colleagues?

What did you learn about an individual child?

What did you learn that you can apply to your work next week?

What do you want to learn more about, and how will you do it?

Learning About Each Child

Mr. Lewis Learns by Watching
1. How did Mr. Lewis gather objective and accurate information about Jessica during a daily routine?
   • *He recorded exactly what he saw Jessica do.*

2. What did Mr. Lewis learn about Jessica?
   • *Jessica is confident about spreading apple butter.*
   • *She uses both hands to complete her task: one hand to hold the bowl and then the bagel, and the other hand to hold and move the spreader.*
   • *She likes apple butter.*

Working as a Team to Offer a Program That Meets Each Child's Needs

Three Colleagues Plan as a Team
1. How did Ms. Bates use a team approach to planning?
   • *She suggested a focus for the next meeting.*
   • *She asked each teacher to focus on outdoor time during the week.*

2. How did the teachers use information from their observations to support individual children and the group?
   • *On the basis of their observations, the teachers decided to get additional materials (more balls) and offer a new activity (washing the wagons).*

Evaluating the Program

Three Colleagues Evaluate Their Program
1. What information did Ms. Gonzalez, Ms. Bates, and Mr. Lewis use to evaluate their program?
   • *They reviewed the children's developmental summary forms.*
   • *They listed activities that worked well and those that presented problems.*

2. On the basis of their evaluation, what did Ms. Gonzalez, Ms. Bates, and Mr. Lewis decide to do?
   • *They will get a new climber and create more space for children who crawl to explore outdoors safely.*
   • *They will make changes to morning greetings and the daily schedule.*

Feedback

You will use this *Feedback Summary* many times as you complete the sections of this module. Feedback is an important part of this training program because it helps you check your understanding, apply knowledge, and build skills. You may seek feedback from your colleagues, your trainer, or members of a child's family. When an *Answer Sheet* is provided, you may also compare your ideas to example answers. Remember that there can be more than one good answer to a question.

This chart lists some feedback sources and provides space for notes. Each time you get feedback, describe, in the appropriate column, how it was provided (e.g., discussing your responses to learning activities, feedback after your interactions with children have been observed, written comments). This will help you remember to get feedback from a variety of sources and in a number of ways.

Section	Source of Feedback				
	Colleague	Trainer	Child's Family	Answer Sheet	Other
Overview					
Viewing Yourself as a Professional					
Pre-Training Assessment					
A. Meeting Professional Standards					
B. Continuing to Gain New Knowledge and Skills					
C. Behaving Ethically in Your Work					
D. Talking About the Value of Your Work					
Reflecting on Your Learning					

Overview

☐ **Answer** the following questions about the three *Overview* stories in module 13 of *Caring for Infants & Toddlers*.

☐ **Compare** your answers to those on the *Answer Sheet* provided in section 13-10.

☐ **Share and get feedback** on your responses. **Chart** your feedback in section 13-1.

When you are finished, read *Viewing Yourself as a Professional* in module 13 of *Caring for Infants & Toddlers*.

Continually Improving Your Performance

Ms. Gonzalez Decides to Organize Her Room

1. How did Ms. Gonzalez assess her own performance?

2. What did she decide to do after her self-assessment?

Continuing to Gain New Knowledge and Skills

Ms. Bates Conducts Online Research

1. What did Ms. Bates learn that can help her support the development of the infants and toddlers in her care?

2. How did Ms. Bates, Mr. Lewis, and Ms. Gonzalez help each other continue to learn about infants and toddlers and best practices?

Behaving Ethically in Your Work

Responding to Ricky in a Positive Way

1. How did Ms. Bates uphold professional ethics when talking with a parent?

2. How did Ms. Bates interact with Ricky in a professional manner?

Viewing Yourself as a Professional

☐ **Think** about what it means to be a professional.

☐ **Consider** the special talents and interests you bring to your work.

☐ **Record** your ideas by completing the sentences below.

☐ **Share and get feedback** on your responses. **Chart** your feedback in section 13-1.

When you are finished, complete section 13-4, *Pre-Training Assessment.*

I am a professional because...

I describe my personality and style in the following ways:

My special interests include...

I can share my special interests with children by...

I am especially good at...

I can share these talents and skills with children by...

Pre-Training Assessment

☐ **Read** this list of strategies that teachers use to enhance their professionalism. Refer to the glossary in *Caring for Infants & Toddlers* if you need definitions of the terms that are used.

☐ **Record** whether you do these things regularly, sometimes, or not enough, by checking the appropriate boxes.

☐ **Review** your answers.

☐ **List** 3–5 skills you would like to improve or topics you would like to learn more about. (When you finish this module, you will list examples of your new or improved knowledge and skills.)

☐ **Share and get feedback** on your responses. **Chart** your feedback in section 13-1.

When you are finished, begin *Learning Activity A, Meeting Professional Standards*, in module 13 of *Caring for Infants & Toddlers*.

Continually Improving Your Performance

check the appropriate box — regularly / sometimes / not enough

	regularly	sometimes	not enough
1. Try new approaches when current practices are not working with individual children or the group.	☐	☐	☐
2. Ask for feedback from families, colleagues, and supervisors.	☐	☐	☐
3. Use professional standards as guidelines for providing high-quality care.	☐	☐	☐
4. Stay healthy by taking care of your physical, emotional, social, and intellectual needs.	☐	☐	☐

Continuing to Gain New Knowledge and Skills

check the appropriate box — regularly / sometimes / not enough

	regularly	sometimes	not enough
5. Participate in professional organizations and staff development opportunities.	☐	☐	☐
6. Keep up-to-date about ways to build positive relationships with infants and toddlers.	☐	☐	☐
7. Observe and talk with colleagues to increase your knowledge and learn new teaching strategies.	☐	☐	☐
8. Work with families, as partners, to understand and respond to children's skills, interests, and needs.	☐	☐	☐
9. Work toward a credential and/or teaching degree.	☐	☐	☐

Pre-Training Assessment, continued

Behaving Ethically in Your Work

check the appropriate box — regularly / sometimes / not enough

10. Maintain confidentiality about children and families. ☐ ☐ ☐

11. Treat each child as an individual and show no bias because of culture, language, background, abilities, or gender. ☐ ☐ ☐

12. Support the use of developmentally appropriate practices and speak out against inappropriate practices. ☐ ☐ ☐

13. Discuss concerns with supervisors and administrators so they can be addressed. ☐ ☐ ☐

14. Support colleagues when they need assistance. ☐ ☐ ☐

Skills to Improve or Topics to Learn More About

☐ **Obtain and read** one of the following publications:

Lally, J. R, Griffen, A., Fenichel, E., Segal, M., Szanton, E. S., & Weissbourd, B. (2003). *Caring for infants and toddlers in groups: Developmentally Appropriate Practice* (2003 ed.). Washington, DC: ZERO TO THREE Press.
(This book may be ordered online from www.zerotothree.org or by calling 800-899-4301.)

Lally, J. R., Torres, Y. L., & Phelps, P. C. (1994, April/May). Caring for infants and toddlers in groups: Necessary considerations for emotional, social, and cognitive development. *Zero to Three, 14*(5), 1–8.
(This article is available online at www.zerotothree.org/bulletin/Vol14-5p.1.pdf)

National Association for the Education of Young Children. *Principles of child development and learning that inform developmentally appropriate practice: Developmentally appropriate practice in early childhood programs serving children from birth through age 8.* Washington, DC: Author.
(This statement is available online at www.naeyc.org/about/positions/dap3.asp)

National Association for the Education of Young Children. *Guidelines for decisions about developmentally appropriate practice: Developmentally appropriate practice in early childhood programs serving children from birth through age 8.* Washington, DC: Author.
(These guidelines are is available online at www.naeyc.org/about/positions/dap3.asp)

☐ **Think** about your practices, considering the main ideas of the publication you read. **Write** a paragraph about one aspect of providing quality care that is particularly meaningful to you. **Explain** how the principles of developmentally appropriate practice are important to what you do every day. An example is given, to assist your thinking.

☐ **Share and get feedback** on your responses. **Chart** your feedback in section 13-1.

When you are finished, begin *Learning Activity B, Continuing to Gain New Knowledge and Skills,* in Module 13 of *Caring for Infants & Toddlers.*

Assessing Your Practice—Example

Publication: *Caring for Infants and Toddlers in Groups: Developmentally Appropriate Practice*

Date: *January 28*

According to Caring for Infants and Toddlers in Groups, *"watching, asking, and adapting are the tools of responsive caregiving." I think that I am good at watching children and getting to know them. I ask myself, "What does this child need from me?" Then I try to be flexible and do my best to meet the child's needs. It isn't easy, and sometimes I can't do it. However, I think the important thing is always to try and to treat children and families with respect.*

Assessing Your Practice

Publication:_____

Date: _____

☐ **Review** the list of early childhood professional organizations provided in *Learning Activity B*, module 13, *Caring for Infants & Toddlers*. **Select** one organization that you would consider joining and **find out** all you can about it. You can use their Web site or toll-free number to get information.

☐ **Develop** a professional development plan that includes short- and long-term goals. For the short term, you might focus on the area that you want to improve first. For the long term, you can build on an area of strength, adding to skills you have already developed. **Identify** available resources, possible barriers to reaching your goals, and ways to overcome difficulties. An example is provided to assist your thinking.

☐ **Share and get feedback** on your responses. **Chart** your feedback in section 13-1.

When you are finished, begin *Learning Activity C, Behaving Ethically in Your Work*, in module 13 of *Caring for Infants & Toddlers*.

An Early Childhood Professional Organization

Name of the organization I want to learn more about:

What I like about this organization:

I plan to use the organization's services to continue to increase my knowledge and skills by *(e.g., becoming a member, attending a conference, regularly checking their Web site, purchasing publications, signing up for an e-newsletter and bulletins)*:

My Professional Development Plan—Example

Date: _____

Short-Term Goals

I want to pursue these short-term goals:

I want to

- *take a course on guiding children's behavior*

- *complete module 8,* Self

To achieve these goals, I can...

- *use the center library*

- *talk with my trainer, supervisor, and other teachers who use positive guidance strategies*

These barriers might hinder me from completing these goals:

- *It's hard to find time to complete learning activities and still care for children.*

- *I might not find anything in the center library about the reasons for children's behavior.*

To overcome these barriers, I can...

- *bring my lunch and use my lunch break twice a week to read about children's behavior and to work on the learning activities*

- *visit the NAEYC and ZERO TO THREE Web sites to see what resources these organizations offer*

Long-Term Goal

I want to pursue this long-term goal:

I will get my infant/toddler child development associate credential within the next three years.

To achieve this goal, I can...

attend classes at the local child care resource and referral agency

These barriers might hinder me from completing this goal:

I'm not sure what I'll have to do, so I'm not sure whether I can do it.

To overcome these barriers, I can...

- *talk with colleagues who have their CDA credential*

- *talk with someone at the resource and referral agency before classes begin, to learn more about what is required*

My Professional Development Plan

Date: _____

Short-Term Goals

I want to pursue these short-term goals:

To achieve these goals, I can...

These barriers might hinder me from completing these goals:

To overcome these barriers, I can...

Long-Term Goal

I want to pursue this long-term goal:

To achieve this goal, I can...

These barriers might hinder me from completing this goal:

To overcome these barriers, I can...

☐ **Review** the list of ethical principles that apply to teaching.

☐ **List** examples of ways that your behavior upholds these principles.

☐ **Share and get feedback** on your responses. **Chart** your feedback in section 13-1.

When you are finished, complete *Learning Activity D, Talking About the Value of Your Work*, in Module 13 of *Caring for Infants & Toddlers*.

Applying Professional Ethics

Ethics of Teaching	Examples of My Professional Behavior
Treat each child as an individual; avoid comparisons; and show no bias because of culture, background, abilities, or gender.	
Be honest, reliable, and regular in attendance.	
Treat families with respect, even in difficult situations.	
Maintain confidentiality about children and their families.	

Ethics of Teaching	Examples of My Professional Behavior
Make sure materials, activities, practices, and routines are developmentally appropriate.	
Be a positive model for learning and language skills. Never use profanity in front of children and families.	
Wear clothes that are appropriate for your work. Pay attention to dress, grooming, and hygiene.	
Maintain accurate, timely, and appropriate records.	
Advocate on behalf of children, families, yourself, and others. Let others know how children benefit from high-quality early childhood programs.	

Learning Activity D
Talking About the Value of Your Work

☐ **Respond** to the questions below by describing the value of your work and your ideas about improving the early childhood field.

☐ **Review** the ideas for talking about the value of your work and advocating for high-quality programs that are suggested in *Learning Activity D*, module 13, *Caring for Infants & Toddlers*.

☐ **Describe** two steps that you feel comfortable taking to advocate for your beliefs. (You may use any of the suggestions or your own ideas.) After taking these actions, **record** the results.

☐ **Share and get feedback** on your responses. **Chart** your feedback in section 13-1.

When you are finished, complete section 13-9, *Reflecting on Your Learning*.

Your Views About the Early Childhood Profession

Describe a time when your program or you, personally, made a very positive difference for a child.

Describe a time when your program or you, personally, made a very positive difference for a family who needed services.

What do you want policy makers and funders to know about the importance of your work with children and families?

If you had the power to improve the working conditions of early childhood teachers, what would you change?

Learning Activity D, continued

Talking About the Value of Your Work

A Commitment to Advocate for the Profession

Advocacy Steps I Will Take	The Result

Reflecting on Your Learning

You have now completed all of the learning activities for this module. Whether you are a new or experienced teacher, you have gained new understandings and developed new professional skills. Before going on to the next module, take a few minutes to reflect on what you have learned. As you complete the steps below, chart your feedback in section 13-1.

☐ **Review** your responses to the *Pre-Training Assessment* for this module and complete section 13-9b, "Summarizing Progress."

☐ **Explore some curriculum connections.** You will use the skills you developed through module 13, *Professionalism*, when implementing a curriculum. Examples of teachers' professional commitment appear throughout *The Creative Curriculum for Infants & Toddlers*. Here are some selections you may find helpful.

- The introductory section, *Why a Curriculum for Infants and Toddlers?*, describes the characteristics of high-quality programs and the relationship of curriculum to high-quality programming.

- Chapter 4, *Community: Building a Network of Support*, includes a discussion of why programs need support, what communities are doing to support families, and ways to advocate for children.

☐ **Build partnerships with families.** Share what you learned in this module with the families of children in your care. Here are some suggestions:

- Share what you learned about why adults are better able to care for children when they also take good care of themselves.

- Tell families how you continue to learn about caring for infants and toddlers. Share some of the resources you use and information you discover.

- Take photographs of children playing. Share them with families and discuss what children are learning through their experiences at the program.

- Include families in an advocacy effort, such as writing letters to a state legislator about a pending issue.

☐ **Complete the assessments.** Tell the trainer who is guiding you through the modules that you are ready for the knowledge and competency assessments.

If this is your last module, you have successfully completed the training program. Congratulations on a job done well!

Reflecting on Your Learning

Summarizing Progress

Name: _____ **Date:** _____

Describe what belonging to the early childhood profession means to you.

What did you learn about the standards of the profession that is helping you the most?

How can you build a partnership with families to advocate for high-quality care and education programs?

What curriculum connections did you explore?

What do you want to learn more about, and how will you do it?

Answer Sheet
Overview

Continually Improving Your Performance

Ms. Gonzalez Decides to Organize Her Room

1. How did Ms. Gonzalez assess her own performance?
   - *She thought about how the day had progressed.*
   - *She thought about how she felt about the day's events.*

2. What did she decide to do as a result of her self-assessment?
   - *She decided to organize the room more effectively.*
   - *She asked Mr. Lewis, another teacher, for some tips.*

Continuing to Gain New Knowledge and Skills

Ms. Bates Conducts Online Research

1. What did Ms. Bates learn that can help her support the development of infants and toddlers?
   - *She learned about an infant/toddler Web site.*
   - *She got ideas for making safe toys.*

2. How did Ms. Bates, Mr. Lewis, and Ms. Gonzalez help each other continue to learn about infants and toddlers and best practices?
   - *They shared their interest and enthusiasm.*
   - *They shared information about making toys and about the Web site.*

Behaving Ethically in Your Work

Responding to Ricky in a Positive Way

1. How did Ms. Bates uphold professional ethics when talking with a parent?
   - *She responded to the parent's comments about Ricky in a positive way.*
   - *She changed the conversation to focus on the parent's child.*

2. How did Ms. Bates interact with Ricky in a professional manner?
   - *She acted quickly to ensure Ricky's safety.*
   - *She used positive guidance techniques to redirect him to a safe place to jump.*